QUICK STUDIES

I Corinthians–Ephesians

DAVID C. COOK PUBLISHING CO.

ELGIN, ILLINOIS—WESTON, ONTARIO

The following authors and editors contributed to this volume:

Stan Campbell
Jane Vogel
John Duckworth
Jim Townsend, Ph.D.

Quick Studies
I Corinthians Through Ephesians

© 1992 David C. Cook Publishing Co.

Published by David C. Cook Publishing Co.
850 North Grove Ave., Elgin, IL 60120
Cable address: DCCOOK
Designed by Bill Paetzold
Cover illustrations by Steve Björkman
Inside illustrations by Michael Fleishman and Jack DesRocher
Printed in U.S.A.

ISBN: 0-7814-0027-9

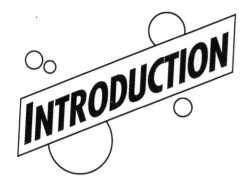

Quick Questions about *Quick Studies*

We've made *Quick Studies* as self-explanatory as possible, so you can dive in and start using them right away. But just in case you were wondering . . .

When should I use *Quick Studies*?
Whenever you want high school or junior high kids to explore the Bible face-to-face and absorb it into their lives. We've kept the openers active and the discussion questions creative, so you can use *Quick Studies* with confidence in Sunday school, midweek youth Bible study, small groups, even youth group meetings and retreats.

What's so quick about *Quick Studies*?
They're designed to save you preparation time. The session plans are compact, for quick reading. There aren't a lot of materials to gather, either (you'll need Bibles, pencils and paper, copies of the reproducible sheets, and sometimes a few other items). Yet *Quick Studies* are *real* Bible studies, with plenty of thought-provoking discussion and life application.

How are these different from other youth Bible studies?
We like to think *Quick Studies* are . . .
• *Irresistible.* You already know most kids don't jump at the chance to fill in a bunch of blanks in a boring study guide. So we used creative, reproducible sheets and *active* activities to draw kids into Scripture.
• *Involving.* You need discussion *starters*, not discussion *stoppers*. We avoided dull "yes or no" questions and included lots of thought-provokers that should get your group members talking about important issues. And we didn't forget suggested *answers* to most of the tougher questions, which should make things easier for you.
• *Inductive.* Many Bible studies try to force-feed kids a single "aim" and ignore other points Scripture is trying to make. *Quick Studies* let kids discover a variety of key principles in a passage.
• *Influential.* It's not enough to know what the Bible says. Every session includes a step designed to help kids decide what to do *personally* with vital points from the chapter.

When do kids read the passages covered?

That's up to you. If your group is into homework, assign the passages in advance. If not, take time to read the Scripture together after the "Opening Act" step that kicks off each session. There are dozens of ways to read a passage—with volunteers taking turns, or with a narrator and actors "performing" a scene, or with kids underlining points as they read silently, or with you reading as the author and kids listening as the original audience, or with small groups paraphrasing as they read . . .

What if I want to cover more—or less—than a chapter in a session?

Quick Studies is flexible. Each 45- to 60-minute session covers a chapter of the New Testament, but you can adjust the speed to fit your group. To cover more than one chapter in a session, just pick the points you want to emphasize and drop the activities, questions, and reproducible sheets you don't need. To cover less than a chapter, you may need to add a few questions and spend more time discussing the "So What?" application step in detail.

Do I have to cover a whole New Testament book?

No. Each session stands alone. Use sessions one at a time if you want to, or mix and match books in any order you choose. No matter how you use them, *Quick Studies* are likely to help your group see Bible study in a whole new light.

John Duckworth, Series Editor

The Best of Boast Worlds

Paul opens his first letter to the church in Corinth with an appeal for unity. He contrasts the "wisdom" of the world with the "foolishness" of Christianity, and he suggests that if we are going to boast about something, we should boast about God.

Cut apart the reproducible sheet, "I Agree." (If you have more than twelve group members, make enough copies so that there is a card for each group member.) Let each person draw a card and read the statement on it. Everyone else should estimate to what extent the person agrees with the opinion, using a scale of 1 (strongly disagrees) to 10 (strongly agrees). Keep score by recording the difference between their estimates and the person's answer in each case. This chapter challenges us to "agree with one another" (vs. 10)—not about silly things, but about one thing of real importance.

DATE I USED THIS SESSION _____ GROUP I USED IT WITH _____

NOTES FOR NEXT TIME _____

_____

_____

1. Think about your best friend (or friends) a minute. What are some of the things you have in common?

2. If you had the job of writing a letter to Christians everywhere (vs. 2), **what would you pick out as the main thing they have in common?** (Compare responses to what Paul says in verse 2: that Jesus Christ is "their Lord and ours.")

3. Think about your friends again. Why are you thankful for them? Can you relate to any of the reasons Paul says thanks for his friends (in vss. 4-9)? **Do you think your friends can see any of those good things in you?** (Draw out ways kids and their friends might show the attributes Paul mentions.)

4. Imagine that you are running for student body president. You've got great ideas (like banning all exams), and lots of people are supporting you. Then you find out that your best friend is running for the same office. How do you feel? (Enjoy the friendly competition; worry that being opponents will hurt your friendship, etc.) **What would you do?** (Go all out and let the best man [or woman] win; drop out of the race; team up for a co-presidency, etc.)

5. How does that situation compare with the one Paul describes in verses 10-12? (The "Paul Fan Club," the "Apollos Fan Club," and others were quarreling.)

6. Based on what he says in verses 10 and 13-17, how do you think Paul felt about the rivalry? (He didn't enjoy the popularity. Clearly he wanted to put an end to it, even if it meant losing his status as a local hero.) **Do you think he was overreacting?** (Paul saw anything that divided the church as dividing Christ, and he didn't want anyone to look up to him the way they should look up to Christ [v. 13].)

7. It might have been easier for the Corinthian Christians to brag about their leaders than to brag about Christianity itself. How many of the examples Paul gives in verses 18-23 still seem a little embarrassing today? (Allow kids the freedom to admit that sometimes Christianity may seem "foolish," and that it might be easier to brag if they had more miraculous signs to show off [vs. 22].)

8. **How have you experienced the power and wisdom of God that Paul talks about in verses 24 and 25?** (Encourage specific examples, and point out that faith is itself evidence, since it takes God's power and wisdom to overrule our objections.)

9. **If you were putting together a church, what kind of people would you choose to be in it? Some of us might choose the smartest, most influential people. But God didn't do it that way. Paul wasn't trying to be rude by what he wrote in verses 26-31. How had Paul already applied those ideas to himself? (Hint: Look back at verses 10-17.)** (Paul emphasized that his abilities as a leader were not the important thing; Christ is.)

10. **Does this passage mean that if you're smart, you can't be a Christian? Or if you're a Christian, you have to get stupid?** (Urge kids to see that the comparison is between our abilities and God's even greater wisdom and power. With that perspective, the only thing we can even think about boasting of is God.)

While some of your group members may benefit from a dose of humility, don't let them leave this chapter thinking that they ought to put down themselves or other Christians. Make concrete the abstract concept of "boasting in the Lord" by explaining that when we boast about ourselves, we draw attention to ourselves. When we boast about God, we draw attention to Him. Invite kids to give specific examples of this by naming "famous" Christians who have used their high profiles to publicly talk about Christ (some sports figures, former President Jimmy Carter, contemporary Christian musicians, etc.). Then brainstorm ways in which group members could do something similar. Ask, for example, **How could Dan brag about his athletic ability? How could he use it to draw attention to God?** (By recognizing it as a gift from God, by "playing clean" and letting others know why, etc.) Try to mention a strength of every group member.

I AGREE

It's OK for girls to ask guys out on dates.

Girls are naturally better students than guys.

Girls should pay their own way on dates, even if the guy does the asking.

Most girls are better drivers than most guys.

A guy looks stupid wearing an earring.

I would never kiss on the first date.

Guys should hold the door for girls (anytime, not just on a date).

If you're under 17, you shouldn't watch an R-rated video.

I would consider dyeing my hair.

Guys can keep secrets better than girls can.

Guys are naturally more athletic than girls.

Girls tend to have closer friendships than guys.

I CORINTHIANS 2

Wise Up

Only by God's Spirit can we understand God's secret wisdom.

Distribute the reproducible sheet, "Wisdom Test," and let kids have fun trying to figure out the brain teasers. [Answers: (1) The first two cuts should divide it into equal fourths, and the third cut is horizontal, through the center; (2) after you cut the cake in half each time, place one half exactly on top of the other before making the next cut; (3) fourteen; (4) move #1 to the left of #2, #10 to the right of #3, and #7 centered beneath #8 and #9; (5) since each day the snail gets two feet higher than he finally stops, on day #28 he will reach the top; (6) ducks; (7) sleeplessness; (8) E, N, and T (for Eight, Nine, and Ten).]

DATE I USED THIS SESSION _____ GROUP I USED IT WITH _____

NOTES FOR NEXT TIME _____

_____

_____

1. Suppose you were going to apply for an after-school job as a salesperson at a clothing store. What qualities do you think you'd need to land the job and be successful at it?

2. Have you ever seen or heard someone try to "sell" religion? In what ways? (Examples: Cult members with memorized pleas; showy TV evangelists who promise "gifts" in exchange for a pledge, etc.)

3. Paul says he purposely didn't use sales techniques to convince people of the Gospel (vss. 1-5). Do you think he was effective because of that, or in spite of it? (According to him, his "secret" was weakness, fear, and much trembling. Yet his words were supported by the wisdom and power of the Holy Spirit.) How might this apply to the way you talk about God to others? (It is much more important to rely on the Holy Spirit than to feel confident in one's own abilities.)

4. Based on what you see and read, what is some of the information you would say is "the wisdom of this age" (vs. 6)? (Examples: Sex should be "safe"; abortion is simply a matter of personal choice; practicing homosexuality is an acceptable alternative lifestyle, etc.)

5. Why do you think so many people are fooled by "wisdom" that isn't really wise (vss. 6-10)? (God's wisdom is available only through the Holy Spirit.)

6. How do you receive the Spirit (vs. 12)? (By receiving Christ. If your church believes in an additional experience of the Holy Spirit, you may want to mention that here. In any case, take this opportunity to make sure your kids know how to belong to Christ.)

7. Two laptop computers can look exactly the same. But if one has a working battery and the other doesn't, it's obvious which one will be "wiser." The Spirit "energizes" us with the mind of Christ so that we can "compute" the spiritual truths that other people miss (vss. 11-16). Are you struggling with any spiritual ideas that you can't quite seem to grasp? If so, what else can you do? (Continue to seek God's help in understanding. Also, it might help to open up some of these things to group discussion. Perhaps others can shed some light for the person who is struggling.)

8. **Does having the wisdom of the Spirit mean you'll automatically get straight *A's* ? If spiritual wisdom doesn't guarantee academic success, what do you think is the main benefit of it?** (True spiritual wisdom means we recognize Christ for who He is and accept His salvation by faith. Then we can begin to see the world from His perspective—with "the mind of Christ." We're also saved from making some painful mistakes if we seek God's priorities in making decisions.)

Brainstorm ways that having "the mind of Christ" gives your group members a different perspective than their unbelieving peers have. (Consider specific moral standards, relationships, attitudes toward parents, etc.) Invite kids to share ways that non-Christians might think this perspective is foolish. Then spend a few minutes discussing whether your group is as "wise" as it should be. Ask a few questions like these: **Would Christ be pleased with our treatment of each other at our meetings? How can we help each person to feel like an important part of the group? Are there other people we should be inviting to attend? What are some recent things we've studied (and learned) that we haven't begun to practice yet?**

W■SDOM TEST

1

How do you cut a regular circular cake into eight equal parts using only three cuts with a knife?

2

There's another correct answer to question #1. What is it?

3

How many triangles are in this figure?

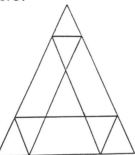

4

Move only three of these circles and turn the triangle upside down.

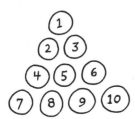

5

A snail is at the bottom of a thirty-foot well. It can crawl upward three feet a day, but at night it slips back two feet. How long does it take the snail to crawl out of the well?

6

A farmer has two eggs for breakfast (at home) every morning. He does not own any hens. He does not buy, beg, or steal the eggs. He does not trade for them. No one gives them to him. Where do the eggs come from?

7

Rearrange these letters to form a common English word:

p n l l e e e e s s s s

8

What are the next three letters in this sequence?

O T T F F S S

A Bunch of Babies

The people in the Corinthian church showed that they were immature and worldly by focusing on the apostles instead of on Christ. He is the only worthwhile foundation for the church, which is pictured as the temple for the Holy Spirit.

(Needed: Baby bottles with juice; jars of baby food; spoons and bibs; prizes [optional])

Explain that you want the girls to "baby" the guys during this activity. Then pull out some baby bottles containing equal amounts of juice (if possible, one for each guy). Have a race to see who will be the first to empty his bottle. The girls are to assist in holding the bottles, since the "babies" are incapable of doing so. Follow with a feeding contest using baby food— girls with jars and spoons, guys with bibs. Baby rattles and toys would make memorable prizes for the winners. (If your group is all guys or all girls, just assign half to be babies and half to be parents.) As silly as this will seem, it can help you make the point that a church full of adults can sometimes act as immature as helpless babies if they stray from the things God expects of them.

DATE I USED THIS SESSION _____ GROUP I USED IT WITH _____

NOTES FOR NEXT TIME _____

_____

_____

1. When was the last time someone treated you as if you were a little kid? How did you feel?

2. Sometimes other people want to treat us as mature adults, but can't because of our immature behavior. Can you think of a time when a parent or teacher trusted you (or a friend) to act in a mature way, and you (or the friend) blew it?

3. Paul wanted to treat the people at Corinth as if they were spiritually mature, but he couldn't (vss. 1-4). **How do you think their immaturity made him feel? How do you think they felt when they read his criticism of them?**

4. The church was being divided because of different personal loyalties—some supported Paul, some Apollos, some other people. But Paul pointed out that each one was only doing his part in the same big job (vss. 5-9). **What examples have you seen of that kind of teamwork—either for a spiritual goal or some other goal?** (On a sports team; in planning a youth group event, etc.)

5. Paul moves from the example of gardening to the example of building (vss. 10-15). **What do you think it means to build using "gold, silver, costly stones" as opposed to "wood, hay, or straw"?** (Some of our actions are much more precious and long-lasting than others, even if the others aren't necessarily bad. Our worthless actions will "go up in smoke," while worthwhile ones will last.)

6. What are some activities you would include as "gold, silver, or costly stones"? What would you classify as "wood, hay, or straw"? (Fun and celebration are valid parts of the Christian life, so don't assume that everything enjoyable is worthless. But the proportion of our fun times to our serious work may need to be examined.)

7. How do you feel about being part of God's temple (vss. 16, 17)? (Note that this reference to God's "temple" is to the church as a whole, in contrast to I Corinthians 6:19, where individuals are pictured as temples.) **What are some of the benefits?** (The Holy Spirit lives in us; God is always with us.) **What are some of the responsibilities?** (We need to be "transparent" enough that others can see God through our lives; we need to make sure we "fit together" as a group and as the church.)

8. **If you're a Christian, how do you think the Holy Spirit felt about living in you last week? Why?**

9. **Just in case all this talk about gold and temples starts giving you a big head, Paul reminds you not to get cocky** (vss. 18-24). **But don't get discouraged either—look how he ends this chapter** (vss. 22, 23)! **What do you think it means that all things are yours?** (Everything worthwhile and lasting [remember vss. 10-15] is available to those who are "of Christ.")

Distribute copies of the reproducible sheet, "This Old Temple." Have two volunteer "actors" read it as others follow along. Then read the verses at the end. Discuss (or just have kids think about): **If our group were a building, what kind of building would it be? How well do we "stick together" as parts of this building? What aspects of our group could use repair? Our relationships? Learning together? Worship? Reaching out to others? Is our foundation really built on Christ, or on something else?**

Cast: Bob Villa, Norm A-Frame

BOB: Hi, and welcome to *This Old Temple*—the show where we look at parts of God's dwelling place and see what we can do to fix them up. I'm Bob Villa, and this is Norm A-Frame.

NORM: Thanks, Bob. Today we have the part of the temple on 16th Street. It's a youth group.

BOB: Wow! It looks a lot older. Those moral supports look like they're about to fall down.

NORM: Whoops! There goes one now. Look out, Bob! Ooh, sorry about your foot.

BOB: That's OK, Norm. I can still hold a hammer. Those bricks in the wall—they look like they could come down at any moment, too.

NORM: Whoops! Here come some now. Sorry about your hands, Bob.

BOB: That's OK. I can still hold some sandpaper in my teeth. But why is this place falling apart?

NORM: Seems all these bricks don't get along with each other. If they don't stick together, the place falls apart,

BOB: Well, let's put this part of the temple in shape for the Lord. What kind of budget do we have?

NORM: Uh . . . eight dollars and fifty cents.

BOB: What? We can't do anything for eight dollars and fifty cents!

NORM: I know. But the bricks spent the rest of the money getting sandblasted.

BOB: I guess they forgot who lives here, eh? *(sighs)* Well, let's—

NORM: Whoops! Here comes a whole wall! Sorry about your head, Bob. *(pause)* Bob? Bob?

"Don't you know that you yourselves are God's temple and that God's Spirit lives in you? If anyone destroys God's temple, God will destroy him; for God's temple is sacred, and you are that temple" (I Corinthians 3:16, 17).

I CORINTHIANS 4

Scum of the Earth

Paul contrasts the faithful, sacrificial work he and the other apostles do with the complacent, boastful attitudes the Corinthians have developed in his absence. He decides to send Timothy to help them—and expresses his own intentions to visit.

(Needed: Several pairs of scissors)

Give each person a copy of the reproducible sheet, "Trophy Traders." Give kids a couple of minutes to cut out their trophies and "money" from the sheet. Then spend the next five to ten minutes letting each person try to put together a better "portfolio" than anyone else, buying and selling trophies for whatever the market will bear. Leave it to each person to decide which trophy is most valuable. Then call a halt to the trading. Let kids show off what they bought and how much money they accumulated. Then tally up the loot by your standard: Everything is worth zero except the "Scum of the Earth" trophy. Tell the group that this chapter will explain this unusual value system.

DATE I USED THIS SESSION _____ GROUP I USED IT WITH _____

NOTES FOR NEXT TIME _____

_____

_____

1. When you think of the word "pastor," what three words come to mind? What three words do you think might come to the mind of someone who doesn't go to church?

2. Do you think your church sees your pastor as a "servant of Christ and . . . [one] entrusted with the secret things of God" (vs. 1)? Why or why not?

3. How could what Paul says about himself in verses 2-5 apply to all Christians? (All Christians have been "given a trust"—salvation, gifts of the Spirit, and more. So the same responsibilities apply.) **To you in particular?** (Do kids have a clear conscience [vs. 4]? Do they worry about what others think of them [vs. 3]? Are they looking forward to praise from God [vs. 5]?)

4. Based on verses 6-8, how do you think Paul was feeling as he wrote this part of the letter? (Angry; frustrated, etc.) **What was he upset about?** (The Corinthians had a problem with pride—thinking of themselves more highly than they should have. Paul reminded them that compared to the apostles, the Corinthians were spiritually "wet behind the ears.")

5. What do you think about sarcastic people? On a sarcasm meter of 1 to 100, what percentage of the time would you say you are sarcastic? (Usually we see sarcasm as a negative thing. But Paul used it to emphasize his point. Have one person read verses 8-10 in a straightforward manner. Then have another person do so with hints of sarcasm in his or her voice, as if he or she were Paul chiding the Corinthian church.)

6. Suppose you read verses 12 and 13 as part of a benefits package in a "Help Wanted" ad in the paper. Would you rush out to apply for the job? Why? Is it fair for God to expect such things from the people who are most dedicated to Him? Explain. (It's not likely the goal of your young people is to achieve the status of "the scum of the earth." We're not unlike the Corinthians in wanting wealth, acceptance, and other comforts. Yet part of being a Christian involves sacrifice. If it seems unfair, remember that Christ was willing to give up even more.)

7. **The Corinthians needed more than a letter; they needed a "personal trainer," so Paul sent Timothy** (vss. 14-17). **Can you think of any people God has provided to help you in your spiritual growth?**

8. **How does your behavior change at school when a teacher leaves the room? If you have a job, how do things change when the boss isn't there? How might a person your age get into trouble if his or her parents left for the weekend? How is this like the problems the Corinthians were having?** (They seemed to think they could get away with anything since Paul wasn't around. Paul decided he needed to go to Corinth in person. [See verses 18-21.] But he hoped the Corinthians could learn to straighten themselves out without his having to use "a whip," so to speak.)

9. **How could you stay faithful to Christ without having someone look over your shoulder all the time?**

Option One: In our society that tends to reject authority and exalt independence, it may seem strange that Paul expected the Corinthians to do what he told them. Ask: **How would people in our church feel if a well-known Christian leader wrote a letter telling us to "shape up"?** (Many people would see it as interference by an outsider.) Challenge each person to name one mature Christian he or she *would* be willing to take direction from. Point out that we make it much harder on ourselves when we try to "go it alone" spiritually. *Option Two:* Plan (or take on right now) a "scummy" service project to do around the church (painting, clean-up, lawn mowing, etc.). Note that service and commitment don't have to be dull and boring chores. If we have the right attitudes, they can even become enjoyable.

TROPHY TRADERS

I CORINTHIANS 5

Guilty by Association

Responding to reports that the Corinthian church condoned a mother/son (or perhaps stepmother/son) sexual relationship, Paul gives a bold command to expel the guilty parties from the church.

(Needed: Hymnals and a tennis ball)

Have group members sit in a circle. Each person holds a hymnal. One person begins by "serving" a tennis ball up and off his or her hymnal, toward another person in the circle. The purpose is to see how many times the group can hit the ball without letting it touch the floor. (No person may hit the ball twice in a row.) Whoever misses, or makes it impossible for someone else to get to the ball, is out. The game can lead into a discussion of what it takes to get kicked out of the church. (If using hymnals in this way would get *you* kicked out of the church, use other books instead.)

DATE I USED THIS SESSION _____ GROUP I USED IT WITH _____

NOTES FOR NEXT TIME_____

_____

_____

1. **How might life be different if there were no such thing as sex?** (Unless people reproduced in another way, none of us would be here; there would probably be no dating or marriage; there would be no sexual temptation; TV shows, movies, and advertising might have to be more creative, etc.)

2. **How does sex affect the church?** (When the church says that sex belongs only in marriage, many people are quick to condemn the church; when church leaders fall into sexual scandals, much damage is done to the credibility of Christianity overall, etc.)

3. **The scandal in Corinth was that a guy was sleeping with his mother—or perhaps his stepmother** (vs. 1). **How do you think you would feel if you attended a church where everyone knew this was taking place? Why?** (Probably uncomfortable. The pastor's ability to speak freely about marital faithfulness might be damaged; outsiders might assume this was a church where "anything goes.") **How did the other Corinthian church members feel about it** (vs. 2)**?** (They were proud, perhaps because they thought they were breaking new ground in "Christian freedom.") **How did Paul feel about it** (vss. 3-5)**?** (He commanded them to immediately expel the guilty man from their fellowship.)

4. **Do you think a person who is so sinful should be in church? Explain.** (If the person were a Christian who wrongly claimed the freedom to go against God's specific instructions, he might negatively influence any number of other people. The purpose of putting such a person out of church was for him to experience the sting of separation from his friends and peers, and to repent. A person who felt no remorse would have nothing to lose by being out in the world.)

5. **Do you know people who use "Christian freedom" as an excuse to sin?** (Example: Some young people are quick to point out that the Bible doesn't come right out and say to abstain from all drinking, so they get drunk from time to time.)

7. Would you say that sexual sin is "minor" in comparison to some others (such as murder or stealing)? Explain. (See verses 6-8. Anytime Christians sin, and especially when the sin is known to others, it has an effect on the whole church.)

8. The world is filled with people who are guilty of some kind of sexual sin. How are we to keep from associating with them all (vss. 9-13)? (We aren't. Non-Christians will act like non-Christians. It is people who profess to be Christians, yet refuse to stop sinning, who can be a threat to the church. Too often we tolerate the sins of "brothers" even as we condemn those sins among "those outside.")

9. Paul's letter was written to a church. How can you apply what he says to yourself? (We may need to give up some of the friendships that tend to bring us down spiritually rather than building us up.)

Hand out copies of the reproducible sheet, "Stay or Go?" The case studies help kids apply the principle mentioned in the last "Q&A" question. Let kids consider the cases in small groups. As you discuss kids' responses, differences of opinions are likely to arise. If not, you should play "devil's advocate" and prevent kids from blandly citing "pat" answers or simply going along with the crowd each time. Follow with a time of prayer, asking God for wisdom to know how long to stay with a shaky relationship and, if necessary, for the courage to walk away from a harmful situation before it's too late.

STAY OR GO ?

How do you know when you'll be a good influence on a non-Christian person or group— and when he, she, or it will be a bad influence on you? When things get hairy, you have to

decide: Do I stick around and keep trying to do some good, or do I leave for my own spiritual health? Decide what you would do in each of the following situations:

1

Against the advice of your parents, you've been dating a non-Christian. This person seems to have opened up to God somewhat since you've been seeing each other. But now every time you go out, you feel pressured to go further sexually than you believe is right. You feel sure the person is close to becoming a Christian, but there's a lot of tension between the two of you as well. Do you maintain the relationship and just try to stay strong, or do you break off the relationship and risk having the other person mad at both you and God?

2

You've been developing a friendship with your science lab partner. He (if you're a guy) or she (if you're a girl) has a pretty wild side, so you were surprised when (s)he asked you if you believed in God (based on something you said in class). You were even more surprised when (s)he said, "For a religious person, you're pretty normal." Your lab partner confessed to feeling messed up over some problems with his or her parents, and you've been thinking maybe you'll get a chance to talk about how God can help. Yesterday (s)he invited you to a party this weekend. Chances are there will be a lot of alcohol and a little of practically everything else—but you don't want to destroy the friendship by seeming judgmental or "abnormal." Maybe you'll get a chance to talk at the party, too. Do you go? Why or why not?

3

Your best friend has been a Christian as long as you've known her. But last month her father was killed by a drunk driver, and your friend is furious at God. She refuses to go to church or youth group. She says terrible things about God—and you—whenever you try to help her see that God is still there for her. You're starting to be affected. You try not to bring up anything about God in your conversation, especially around her. Her frustration with God is making you wonder about Him, too, and you don't feel like praying or reading the Bible anymore. But you really care about your friend and don't want to bail out on her when she's trying to cope with her dad's death. What do you do?

I CORINTHIANS 6

So Sue Me

Paul explains two things that should set Christians apart from the rest of the world: We don't fight each other in court, and we don't make "love" to each other outside of marriage.

Cut apart copies of the reproducible sheet, "Friend or Foe?" Give each group member a card, warning him or her not to let anyone see it. Read the game directions at the top of the sheet, and then let kids play the game. When they've figured out the secret, explain that Paul warns Christians about acting like enemies when they should be on the same team.

DATE I USED THIS SESSION _____ GROUP I USED IT WITH _____

NOTES FOR NEXT TIME _____

_____

_____

1. Have you heard of any lawsuits that seemed crazy or a waste of time? Give an example. (Possibilities: A child suing to "divorce" his parents; a lawsuit over whether musicians sang live or lip-synched at concerts, etc.)

2. Paul thought the idea of Christians suing each other over being "cheated" (vs. 7) was wrong (vss. 1-6). What might unbelievers think if they see Christians going to court against each other? (When Christians take each other to a secular court, they may seem to be denying the authority of the church, or to be unforgiving or unloving. Unbelievers might also think that someone who doesn't have a godly perspective is better equipped to resolve conflict than those who should have the wisdom and Spirit of God.)

3. So if you have a problem with another Christian, what could you do? (Find a third Christian whom you both trust and let him or her decide the matter.)

4. How do you feel about what Paul says in verses 7 and 8—that it's better to let yourself be cheated than to sue? (According to Paul, it's improper to make a big fuss over material things. If we do, he says we're the losers.)

5. When was the last time someone cheated you? What did you do? What's the biggest conflict you've ever "let go" because you thought it more important to keep the peace than to demand your "rights"? How did the incident affect your relationship with the other person? (If the relationship is damaged or destroyed, perhaps the person didn't actually "let go" to the extent he or she thinks.)

6. On a scale of 1 (least) to 10 (most), how severe do you feel the following sins are: Idolatry? Adultery? Male prostitution? Homosexuality? Stealing? Calling people names? Greed? Drunkenness? Swindling? (Explain that while we sometimes think in terms of "little" and "big" sins, Paul put the previous things in the same list of reasons that people miss out on the kingdom of God [vs. 9-11].)

7. The people in Corinth seemed to think that because they were Christians, any behavior was OK for them (vs. 12). **Paul was as big on Christian freedom as anyone** (see Romans 14), **but he could not overlook blatant sin. And he knew that some things can become our masters if we aren't careful. Can you think of any examples?** (We can get "hooked" on certain foods, video games, etc. While some are not wrong in themselves, such things can control huge amounts of our time and energies.)

8. **One of the strongest pressures we feel is to have sex before marriage. If people really took seriously what Paul says in verses 13-20, do you think they would be less likely to be sexually immoral?** (Help group members understand that when we sin, it is as if we carry Jesus into that sin with us.) **How seriously do you take this warning?**

9. **This chapter begins with lawsuits and ends with sleeping around. What's the connection?** (Too often Christians act like all the nonbelievers in the world—as if Jesus had made no difference in their lives. We should be different in that Christ is our standard.)

Our disobedient actions take on new significance if we think in terms of taking Jesus along with us in whatever we do. Ask kids what they think Jesus would do in the following situations: (a) Getting punched by a kid who hates "foreigners"; (b) walking into a convenience store and seeing a rack of pornographic magazines behind the counter; (c) being asked by a friend to make an illegal copy of a movie rented from the video store. Then ask: **How do you think Jesus would feel about having to fight "through your hands" with a kid who hit you? How would He feel about having to watch "through your eyes" as you stare at those magazines as long as you can? How would He feel about having "His" hands used to make an illegal copy of a videotape?** Then brainstorm some activities that kids think Christ would *like* to join them in this week.

FRIEND OR FOE ?

To the leader: Give each player one card, warning each to keep the contents secret. Then give these instructions:

Your job is to find the other players who are on your side without getting "killed" by your enemies on the other side. Read your card carefully to yourself without letting anyone else see it. Follow those instructions exactly when you approach someone or when someone approaches you. If a person says, "I am a friend," put your hands on his or her shoulders and follow him or her around. If a person says, "I am a foe," you are "dead" and must fall to the ground immediately and stay there for the rest of the game.

Do *not* let kids know that they all have the same passwords and therefore are all on the same side.

When you approach someone, say: The ducks in Paris are fine this year. **If the person says:** But the geese in Madrid are fatter, **you say:** I am a friend. **If the person says:** I hate Paris this time of year, **you say:** I am a foe. **If someone approaches you and says:** The ducks in Paris are fine this year, **you say:** But the geese in Madrid are fatter. **If someone approaches you and says anything else, you say:** I am a foe.

When you approach someone, say: The ducks in Paris are fine this year. **If the person says:** But the geese in Madrid are fatter, **you say:** I am a friend. **If the person says:** I hate Paris this time of year, **you say:** I am a foe. **If someone approaches you and says:** The ducks in Paris are fine this year, **you say:** But the geese in Madrid are fatter. **If someone approaches you and says anything else, you say:** I am a foe.

When you approach someone, say: The ducks in Paris are fine this year. **If the person says:** But the geese in Madrid are fatter, **you say:** I am a friend. **If the person says:** I hate Paris this time of year, **you say:** I am a foe. **If someone approaches you and says:** The ducks in Paris are fine this year, **you say:** But the geese in Madrid are fatter. **If someone approaches you and says anything else, you say:** I am a foe.

When you approach someone, say: The ducks in Paris are fine this year. **If the person says:** But the geese in Madrid are fatter, **you say:** I am a friend. **If the person says:** I hate Paris this time of year, **you say:** I am a foe. **If someone approaches you and says:** The ducks in Paris are fine this year, **you say:** But the geese in Madrid are fatter. **If someone approaches you and says anything else, you say:** I am a foe.

When you approach someone, say: The ducks in Paris are fine this year. **If the person says:** But the geese in Madrid are fatter, **you say:** I am a friend. **If the person says:** I hate Paris this time of year, **you say:** I am a foe. **If someone approaches you and says:** The ducks in Paris are fine this year, **you say:** But the geese in Madrid are fatter. **If someone approaches you and says anything else, you say:** I am a foe.

When you approach someone, say: The ducks in Paris are fine this year. **If the person says:** But the geese in Madrid are fatter, **you say:** I am a friend. **If the person says:** I hate Paris this time of year, **you say:** I am a foe. **If someone approaches you and says:** The ducks in Paris are fine this year, **you say:** But the geese in Madrid are fatter. **If someone approaches you and says anything else, you say:** I am a foe.

When you approach someone, say: The ducks in Paris are fine this year. **If the person says:** But the geese in Madrid are fatter, **you say:** I am a friend. **If the person says:** I hate Paris this time of year, **you say:** I am a foe. **If someone approaches you and says:** The ducks in Paris are fine this year, **you say:** But the geese in Madrid are fatter. **If someone approaches you and says anything else, you say:** I am a foe.

When you approach someone, say: The ducks in Paris are fine this year. **If the person says:** But the geese in Madrid are fatter, **you say:** I am a friend. **If the person says:** I hate Paris this time of year, **you say:** I am a foe. **If someone approaches you and says:** The ducks in Paris are fine this year, **you say:** But the geese in Madrid are fatter. **If someone approaches you and says anything else, you say:** I am a foe.

When you approach someone, say: The ducks in Paris are fine this year. **If the person says:** But the geese in Madrid are fatter, **you say:** I am a friend. **If the person says:** I hate Paris this time of year, **you say:** I am a foe. **If someone approaches you and says:** The ducks in Paris are fine this year, **you say:** But the geese in Madrid are fatter. **If someone approaches you and says anything else, you say:** I am a foe.

When you approach someone, say: The ducks in Paris are fine this year. **If the person says:** But the geese in Madrid are fatter, **you say:** I am a friend. **If the person says:** I hate Paris this time of year, **you say:** I am a foe. **If someone approaches you and says:** The ducks in Paris are fine this year, **you say:** But the geese in Madrid are fatter. **If someone approaches you and says anything else, you say:** I am a foe.

The Facts of Life

The best way to prevent sexual immorality is to understand God's perspective on love, sex, marriage, and divorce. While Paul apparently had chosen not to marry, and was quite happy to have the freedom to devote all his time to God, he also talks about the benefits of strong marriages and provides some guidelines.

(Partition or other way of isolating someone)

Create your own version of "The Dating Game." Isolate a girl, and then select three guys at random who will answer her questions (or vice versa). Answerers will need to either disguise their voices or write down their responses for someone else to read aloud. After the questioner asks five or six questions, have him or her select his or her most likely dating prospect from the three. (If your group is all one sex, parody the game by having volunteers play members of the opposite sex.) Then remind kids that many people forget to consider one of the most important aspects of a relationship: shared faith.

DATE I USED THIS SESSION _____ GROUP I USED IT WITH _____

NOTES FOR NEXT TIME _____

_____

_____

1. When you think of your future, do you envision yourself as being married or single? Why?

2. Paul was glad to be single. What would you expect his views on marriage to be? (Compare student answers to verses 1-7. He was a big advocate for marriage—and sex within that context.)

3. Do you think Paul, who may have never married or had sex, could really understand how you or others feel when you're with a special person? Explain. (Paul fully understood feelings of passion [vss. 8, 9]. But just as he chose to spend his life spreading the Gospel rather than having a cushy job, he chose to keep his own feelings under control and devote himself to God rather than to a wife and family.)

4. How does Paul's view of divorce (vss. 10-16) compare to how most people look at divorce today? (According to Paul, when a non-Christian married to a Christian wants to leave the marriage, the Christian spouse should allow it. Otherwise, he says, divorce should not be an option.)

5. What are the good things about being single? What are the drawbacks? What are the good things about being married? What are the minuses? (Compare responses with verses 25-28.)

6. Do you think it would be easier to serve God as a single person or as a married couple (vss. 29-35)? Explain. (The main difference is that making a marriage work is a priority that takes a lot of time. Single people usually can devote more time to ministry.)

7. Look at verses 17-24. How could you explain what this means for us without mentioning slavery or circumcision? (We're to be content with where God has put us and do all we can for Him there. If you can "better" yourself, go for it! But be content at each step along the way.)

8. Does this chapter make you want to stay single or get married? Why?

9. Since you may not be on the verge of getting married, how might this chapter apply in the following dating situation? Eddie and Maria have been going together for almost a year. They're both Christians; they go to church and the youth group, but that's about all the "Christian stuff" they seem to have time for. What are some things they could do together that could come under the heading of "serving God"? If they don't start now, what will their lives probably be like if and when they get married?

Get kids thinking about issues raised in I Corinthians 7 with the reproducible sheet, "Thoughts of Love." This will give group members the opportunity to express opinions about some subjects mentioned in this chapter. Encourage honesty; it's OK if you don't have all the answers right now. Spend some time discussing questions that arise from this exercise. Leave some questions for future meetings if needed.

THOUGHTS OF LOVE

Here are a few statements dealing with issues raised in I Corinthians 7. In each case, circle a number to show how much you agree with the statement.

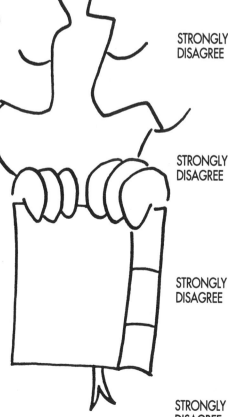

It's better to get a divorce than to stay in a "dead-end" marriage.

STRONGLY DISAGREE  STRONGLY AGREE

Being single is more exciting than being married.

STRONGLY DISAGREE  STRONGLY AGREE

Marriage is something people made up, so they can change the rules about it anytime.

STRONGLY DISAGREE  STRONGLY AGREE

It's OK for Christians to marry non-Christians.

STRONGLY DISAGREE  STRONGLY AGREE

When parents divorce, there's no long-lasting, negative effect on the kids.

STRONGLY DISAGREE  STRONGLY AGREE

Single people can serve God better than married people can.

STRONGLY DISAGREE  STRONGLY AGREE

If you're thirty years old and single, there must be something wrong with you.

STRONGLY DISAGREE  STRONGLY AGREE

People who have boyfriends, girlfriends, or spouses are exempt fom serving God.

STRONGLY DISAGREE 1 2 3 4 5 6 7 8 9 10 STRONGLY AGREE

I CORINTHIANS 8

The Good, the Bad, And the Gray

Paul balances Christian freedom with the challenge to avoid causing "stumbling blocks" for those with a "weak conscience."

(Needed: Objects to hold up)

Designate three corners of the room as "GOOD," "BAD," and "NEUTRAL." Then hold up (or just mention) several items, one at a time. As you hold up each item, kids should move to the designation they feel describes it. Try to include items like a rock music tape or CD, a videocassette, the Bible, a newspaper, a deck of cards, a "loud" shirt, a bag of potato chips, a dollar bill, etc. Discuss kids' reactions. Then explain that in *most* cases objects are neutral. It's our use of those objects that should be classified "good" or "bad."

DATE I USED THIS SESSION _____ GROUP I USED IT WITH _____

NOTES FOR NEXT TIME_____

_____

_____

1. Have you ever eaten something that made you uncomfortable as you ate it—because you weren't sure you should be eating it, or because you wondered how your body would react to it? (Examples: A kind of food you'd never had before; food which might or might not have "gone bad," etc.) **What happened?**

2. The people in Corinth were uncomfortable over eating meat that had been sacrificed to false gods. If you were there and someone offered a big slab of prime rib bought on discount because it had just been offered to the glory of Zeus, would you as a Christian feel comfortable eating it? **Why?** (Some people may quickly justify it based on price and opportunity alone, but make sure they deal with the issue of whether the *real* God would think such a meal was OK.)

3. What was Paul's official verdict about meat sacrificed to other gods (vss. 1-6)? (None of these "gods" were real, so it was no big deal to eat the meat and continue to worship the one true God with a clear conscience.)

4. Does Paul contradict himself when he says that food offered to idols is "defiled" (vs. 7, 8)? **Explain.** (What Paul is saying is that, even though the action is neutral, if you think it's wrong to do it, then it *is* wrong for you—because you are willfully choosing what you believe to be disobedience. Spend some time explaining this sometimes confusing concept so that kids don't always assume that the opposite is true: If you think something's right, that automatically makes it right.)

5. Paul urged the Corinthians not to eat that meat around people who might fall into sin because of it (vss. 9-13). **How do you think people could fall into sin by seeing someone else eat meat offered to idols?** (People who believe it's wrong might be tempted to join in, even though they still don't understand the reason for it. They would be like the people you just discussed, going against their consciences for the wrong reasons.)

6. Do you think it's fair to ask people not to do something just because other people might think it's wrong? Isn't

that hypocritical? (It may not be fair, but it's the loving thing to do. Paul figured giving something up was a pretty small sacrifice to make if it kept him from hurting a "weak brother, for whom Christ died.")

7. **Does this mean we should never do anything that might offend anybody? Explain.** (We shouldn't do things that we know might cause others—the "weak brother"—to sin. This may not be the case when a "stronger" fellow Christian wants to impose a self-made list of rules on us. This is what happened with Jesus, who offended the religious leaders of His day. Still, the overriding principle is love—and it isn't loving to antagonize fellow believers by flaunting our freedom "in their faces.")

8. **How do you think most people would react to Paul's statement in verse 13? Are you willing to say something like that? Explain.**

9. **The meat-offered-to-idols issue may not apply to us, but the command Paul gives still holds true. To what controversies might we need to apply this advice?** (This issue is explored further on the reproducible sheet. Add kids' responses to the list on the sheet.)

The reproducible sheet, "Comfort Zones," will provide group members with more contemporary examples of exercising Christian freedom. In each case, they will need to determine both how comfortable they feel in participating in the action, and how much it might alarm other Christians who observe. Add other issues kids feel are important, too. After some discussion, create role plays based on some of the issues—in which someone who feels the actions are OK is confronted by someone who disagrees. It's one thing to express an opinion, but when forced to talk with someone on the "other side," new considerations may come to light. Be sure to remind kids, just to be safe, "When in doubt, don't do it."

COMFORT ZONES

Sometimes it's easy to know what's right and what's wrong. When we feel like nuking someone who disagrees with us, we suspect that would be wrong. We know not to strap little brother to a sled and send him down "Dead Man's Hill." But other things are not so clear. In each of the following cases, first indicate how comfortable you would be doing the action (writing an "M" for "Me" somewhere on the line). Then estimate how you think the others mentioned (writing "O" for others) would feel if they saw you doing the action.

1. Your favorite musician has come out with a song he calls, "I Love Satan," which is causing quite a controversy. You feel that the lyrics are meant to be tongue-in-cheek, and that the song actually ridicules anyone who gets involved in all that satanist garbage. Yet, based entirely on the title, many of the Christians in town are holding massive protests and calling for all "real Christians" to get rid of their copies of the song. How comfortable would you be with keeping and listening to the song? And how comfortable would other Christians you know be with your keeping it?

**NOT AT ALL
COMFORTABLE**   **COMPLETELY
AT EASE**

2. Your family sends you to pick up a carry-out order at a local restaurant. You don't know it, but the Take-Out section is located in the bar area. You order a root beer to drink while you wait, and the bartender gives it to you in a beer mug. Everyone around you is tossing back drinks, talking loudly, and having a good time. Indicate how you personally would feel in this situation, and how you think people from your church might feel if they happened to see you in this setting.

**NOT AT ALL
COMFORTABLE**   **COMPLETELY
AT EASE**

3. A family from Africa has recently moved into your neighborhood. They hear that your family members are Christians and invite you over for dinner, because they have recently converted to Christianity through the work of a missionary couple. At dinner, they proudly serve an authentic African meal, which includes a drink that is fermented—the equivalent of homemade beer. How comfortable would you be in drinking it? How comfortable do you think your church officials would be if they saw you?

**NOT AT ALL
COMFORTABLE**   **COMPLETELY
AT EASE**

What are some other areas where your personal opinions might conflict with those of other Christians?

I CORINTHIANS 9

Go the Distance

As an apostle, Paul deserved—but never demanded—support for his hard work. Every believer should follow Paul's example of purpose and perseverance as we "run in such a way as to get the prize."

Play a couple of relay races (egg-on-a-spoon, wheelbarrow race, etc.) that your group will find fun—and especially silly. Then ask: **How seriously did you take these races? What are some of the differences between these games and how real runners view their competitions?** (They would train, concentrate, hope for a win and a prize.) Explain that this chapter tells us not to "play" at our Christian life, but to recognize it as challenging—and rewarding for those who stick it out.

DATE I USED THIS SESSION _____ GROUP I USED IT WITH _____

NOTES FOR NEXT TIME_____

_____

_____

1. How do you feel when you do a big favor for someone, but he or she doesn't even seem to care or notice? Do you keep doing favors for the person? Do you keep reminding the person, "You owe me one"? Or what?

2. If your efforts have been overlooked, you should relate to Paul. His "favor" for the Corinthians was to tell them about Jesus and help them become Christians. Yet afterward, some of them even questioned his right to be an apostle (vss. 1-3). How would you have felt in his place? How would you have responded to their charges?

3. If you were one of the Corinthians hearing Paul's arguments in verse 3-11, would you have been convinced that Paul deserved your support? Do you think you would have been getting out your wallet?

4. Paul's explanation led up to the point where many TV evangelists would encourage viewers to sit down and write a check. But Paul made no such request. Would you be willing to give up a salary for the "reward" Paul counted on (vss. 12-18)?

5. How do you suppose Paul became "all things to all men" (vss. 19-23)? (He identified closely with whomever he was talking to. If he was speaking to a Jewish audience, he would talk about his Jewish upbringing and show that he could relate to them. If speaking to someone else, he might use a different approach.)

6. How could you learn to identify more closely with the following people in order to tell them about Jesus: (a) Someone of another race who goes to your school; (b) an elderly lady who lives next door to you; (c) a cousin who is blind; (d) a student who comes from a devout Muslim family? What's one thing you might have in common with each of these people?

7. Do you think Paul's "all things to all people" strategy was ethical? Or was it a shady sales tactic? (It would be wrong if he compromised the truth of the Gospel, but he didn't. It's only logical to look for common bonds by which we can help others see how God's truth relates to them.)

8. Sometimes it may seem that we just drift through life, bothering with our spiritual lives only when we happen to get around to it. How does Paul's description of the Christian life (vss. 24-27) make you feel?

9. On a scale of 1 (least) to 10 (most), how would you rate yourself on:

• being a disciplined person (diet, exercise, study habits, etc.);
• being a hard worker;
• finishing what you start?

10. Based on your ratings, how well will you "run in such a way as to get the prize"? What adjustments might you need to make in your habits so you'll be a better "runner"?

Have three kids act out the skit on the reproducible sheet, "Post-Game Interview." Then ask: **Do you think most Christian kids are more like Bo (players) or like Wimp (spectators)? Why? Does the idea of getting a "reward" from God interest you, or would you rather try to coast and barely make it over the finish line? Are you "in training" or "just watching" in the following areas: (a) Finding out what the Bible says; (b) showing non-Christians what Jesus can do for them; (c) showing others in this group that you care about them; and (d) standing up to temptation? What do you think Paul would have to say about your prospects of winning the "championship"?**

Post-Game Interview

Cast: Brent Mustardburger,
Bo Jockson,
Wimp Chamberlain

BRENT: This is Brent Mustardburger for NBCBS Sports. As you just saw, the biggest game in basketball is now history. What a contest— 143 to 141! I'm here in the locker room with Bo Jockson, whose performance tonight broke every record in the book. Bo, how did you feel going into the game?

BO: Well, Brent, I—

WIMP: *(pushing his way into the interview):* Brent, I felt good. I knew I could take those guys with my legs tied behind my back.

BRENT: Hey, I'm trying to interview Bo Jockson. Who are you?

WIMP: I'm Wimp Chamberlain. Yeah, Brent, this is a fine ball club. I'm just pleased to have had such a big part in tonight's win.

BRENT: What part? I don't remember seeing you on the court.

WIMP: Well, I wasn't exactly on the court.

BRENT: You were on the bench?

WIMP: Well, no. But I was 100 percent behind this ball club.

BRENT: How *far* behind?

WIMP: I was home, watching the game on TV.

BRENT: What are you doing here? This is the players' locker room.

WIMP: Well, there's no need to be so exclusive about it. I set some records tonight, too, you know.

BRENT: Oh, yeah? Like what?

WIMP: I ate six turkey-and-banana sandwiches. And twelve bags of chips. Not those little snack bags. I mean the big ones!

BRENT: So what? The spotlight's on the team, not on you. Players like Bo trained hard for months, even years. All you did was sit and watch and eat potato chips.

WIMP: Not just potato chips. I had cheese curls, too.

BRENT: Get out of my way, Wimp. Bo, tell me—

WIMP: You mean you have to work and sweat and give things up if you want the championship trophy and the TV interviews?

BRENT: That's right.

WIMP: That's not fair! I'm going back to my living room!
(He exits.)

BRENT: Bo, how could anybody be so dumb?

BO: Bo don't know.

I CORINTHIANS 10

Take the Next Exit

God knows what we're capable of and helps us withstand anything we face. Historically, God's people have not done well when tempted; but now, thanks to Jesus, strength is available to do everything to the glory of God.

Before the meeting, cut the signs from the reproducible sheet, "Move It!" Arrange your chairs in a circle and tape a sign to the seat of each chair. (If you have more than fifteen chairs, make more than one set of signs; even if you have fewer than fifteen group members, try to set up fifteen chairs.) See what happens when kids arrive. Do they have trouble finding a seat for which they "qualify"? When all kids have had a chance to see the signs, discuss. This should be an enjoyable way for kids to see that they are not alone in their temptations.

DATE I USED THIS SESSION _____ GROUP I USED IT WITH _____

NOTES FOR NEXT TIME _____

_____

_____

1. Has anyone ever traced your family tree several generations into the past? Were any famous or infamous relatives discovered? If so, what was the reaction to this discovery? (It's strange how excited some people get to discover that they are related to Billy the Kid, Jesse James, or some other famous person—even if the person is notorious.)

2. The Jews were very proud of their history—of Abraham, Moses, Esther, David, the prophets, etc. Yet tucked between the stories of these heroes were a lot of stories about people who were stubborn and disobedient to God. Which ones does Paul mention? (Those mentioned by Paul in verses 1-10 refer to Exodus 32, Numbers 25:1-9, Numbers 21:4-9, and Numbers 16:41-50.) **Why do you think these stories are important enough to be in the Bible?** (One reason is that they're supposed to be warnings for us [vss. 6, 11, 12]. Some people learn from positive examples, but many need more severe warnings before they'll change their behavior. We need to learn from both.)

3. Do you think the Corinthians found verse 13 encouraging (because it promises help) or discouraging (because it leaves no excuse for giving in to temptation)? How about you?

4. What temptations have you faced today? This week?

5. How has God helped you through a recent temptation? Or do you usually give in before God has the opportunity to show you a way around it?

6. Corinth contained a lot of temples to gods and goddesses, so idolatry was a big temptation—especially for people who were recent converts to Christianity (vss. 14-22). We don't face the temptation to offer a goat to Apollo, yet we may spend a lot of money or energy on things that are harmful or that come between ourselves and God. Can you think of examples? (Cigarettes; video rentals of crude movies; rock albums whose artists get more "listening" time than God does, etc.)

7. The Corinthians were a lot like us—a bit confused as to exactly how far they could take their Christian freedom (vss. 23-30). They figured that "everything is permissible," but Paul explained that not everything is beneficial. **What does that mean?** (Certain things may not be on a Bible list of sins, but they may be a waste of time—or they may hinder others' relationship with God.) **What are some things that may be OK, but not constructive?** (Look for examples of "rights" we should give up if they would hinder others.)

8. Could you do the following "for the glory of God" (vss. 31-33): (a) Drive faster than the speed limit; (b) go on a diet, even though you aren't overweight; (c) get a haircut that your parents don't like; (d) "make out" with your girlfriend/boyfriend? Why or why not?

9. Paul writes, "I try to please everybody in every way" (vs. 33). **Is that possible? Is it like "following the crowd," being "a doormat," or something else? Explain.** (Paul meant that he tried not to hurt people who were more sensitive about certain things [like eating meat that had been offered to idols] than he was. He did it not to be popular, but to keep from being a "stumbling block" between anyone and God.) **What possible "stumbling block" would be hardest for you to give up for the sake of someone else? Why?** (Examples: Going to horror movies; making "clever" comments that some think are cruel, etc.)

Help kids practice looking for ways out of temptation. Brainstorm the "top ten" temptations teenagers in your area face. Then brainstorm ways in which God could be providing a way out. (Example: If the temptation is to want something so much that you're willing to steal it, ways out could include earning money to buy the item; paying more attention to the things God *has* given you; staying away from the place where you'd be most tempted to steal the item; telling an older Christian about the temptation, so that you won't be able to keep your theft a secret if he or she sees you with the item, etc.) Pray together that you'll watch for the "exits" God provides—and that you'll be willing to take them.

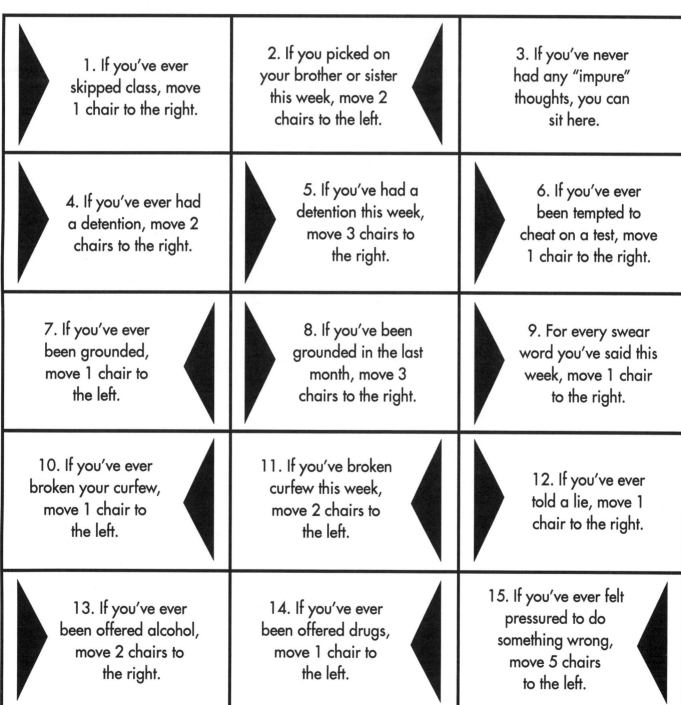

I CORINTHIANS 11

Table Manners

Meaningful worship should be the goal of every church service, so it is important to have a proper sense of order. We should attend with proper dress and appearance, not trying to attract attention to ourselves. Unity is essential. And the Lord's Supper is to help us remember Jesus until His return, so it should be experienced reverently.

Give group members five minutes to find an object that symbolizes something about their relationship with God. (For example, a picture of a friend that someone keeps in her billfold could symbolize how Jesus is her best friend; some-one who feels especially close to God when outdoors could find a leaf.) Explain your own symbol as you give the directions to start kids thinking. After everyone has shared, explain that this chapter talks about a symbol Christ gave us to remind us of Him: the Lord's Supper.

DATE I USED THIS SESSION _____ GROUP I USED IT WITH _____

NOTES FOR NEXT TIME _____

_____

_____

1. Describe a church service you've attended where you found it hard to worship. What was the problem? (Examples: An unfamiliar worship style; crying babies; people whispering nearby; being too sleepy from staying up the night before, etc.)

2. Using a 1 (least) to 10 (most) scale, what would you say is your average level of involvement in the worship service when you go to church?

3. How do you think the people in our church would respond if a woman with a shaved head attended and sat in the front? Do you think more of them would focus on the sermon, or on the shiny head? (Compare to Paul's comments in verses 5 and 6. Explain that in Paul's culture, a shaved head indicated shame and disgrace. He used this image to describe the impact of women who refused to conform to accepted standards of dress during worship.)

4. Some people believe that verses 1-16 are addressed specifically to the culture of Paul's day. Others feel they still apply. How do you feel about the following statements? Why do you think Paul made them?

• "The head of every man is Christ . . ."
• "The head of the woman is man . . ."
• "A woman . . . should cover her head. A man ought not to cover his head . . ."
• "In the Lord, however, woman is not independent of man, nor is man independent of woman."
• "If a man has long hair, it is a disgrace to him . . . if a woman has long hair, it is her glory . . ."

5. Whether all the instructions in verses 1-16 are for today or not, what is the point we shouldn't miss? (Church is not the place to draw attention to yourself. We're all supposed to be submissive to Jesus.)

6. Does this mean that if someone shows up in unusual clothing, hair styles, etc., he or she should be turned away? Explain. (We are not to judge or to show favoritism based on appearance. [See James 2:1-4.] Paul's comments seem directed to people who were established members and knew what was expected, yet who set out to be noticed—not new people who might not have known better.)

7. **What most churches today practice as the Lord's Supper is different from the way it was during the first century. Jesus had established it at a** *meal,* **so the early churches carried on this practice. What would you think of a church that observed the Lord's Supper as Paul describes it in verses 17-22?** (Perhaps group members will agree that, no matter what the form, with problems like this it can't really be the Lord's Supper [vs. 20].)

8. **How does your church practice what Paul teaches in verses 23-26?**

9. **What does the Lord's Supper usually make you think about? Do you ever find yourself just going through the motions?** (Discuss the importance of "examining oneself" each time we participate. [See vss. 27-32.])

10. **Paul tells the Corinthians not to come to church for the food** (vss. 33, 34). **What are some reasons people go to church today, rather than to worship?** (To socialize with friends; to be able to come at other times for basketball, volleyball, or some other activity, etc.) **How do you feel about that?**

Distribute copies of the reproducible sheet, "View from Above." Let kids fill in the thought balloons and complete the picture. Then brainstorm ideas for making group members' worship truly pleasing to God. If your church has specific expectations for those who will take part in the Lord's Supper, you may want to discuss them, too.

How do you think Jesus felt when He saw the Corinthians trashing His supper? Fill in here what His thoughts might have been.

VIEW FROM
ABOVE

Now draw yourself in your typical worship attitude. How does Jesus feel about that? Fill in what you think His thoughts might be.

I CORINTHIANS 12

Rev It Up

The challenge of working together as Christians is to achieve unity, but this is done by being different. God provides "gifts" for each individual. As each person uses his or her unique gifts, the church as a whole is strengthened. Rather than striving to be like someone else, we should discover what we do well and put those abilities to work.

(Needed: Prize [optional])

Before the session, cut the cards from a copy of the reproducible sheet, "Motor City Mismatch." Cut each card in half, placing the left halves in one pile and the right halves in another. When the session begins, have a volunteer come to the front and choose one slip from each face-down pile—coming up with a combination like "stainless steel airbag" or "carpeted gas tank." The volunteer must then try to convince the group in thirty seconds that this feature is a great thing to have on a car. Then repeat the process with as many volunteers as you like, shuffling the piles of slips if needed. (If someone chooses a too-easy combination like "glass windshield," have him or her choose again.) Award a prize for the most convincing salesperson if you like. Then explain that you'll be talking about special abilities God gives people in the church. If the jobs we do in the church don't match our gifts, we're in for trouble.

DATE I USED THIS SESSION _____ GROUP I USED IT WITH _____

NOTES FOR NEXT TIME _____

_____

_____

1. When you get a great gift, what's the first thing you do? Why? (Thank the giver; put it to use right away; show it to others, etc.)

2. With some of the gifts we get, we find a set of instructions. This chapter of Corinthians is the "instruction sheet" for the spiritual gifts we receive from God. What examples can you give of people who have and use one or more of the gifts listed in verses 1-11? (Be prepared to discuss your church's understanding of miracles and speaking in tongues.)

3. Paul uses the example of a body to explain how all this "differentness" can result in unity (vss. 12-27). What other examples can you give of how it's possible to work together, even when the "parts" are very different? (A team with different positions; a machine with different parts, etc.)

4. What are some talents other people have that you wish you had? (Examples: A good singing voice; athletic ability; ease in meeting and talking to new people, etc.) **Is it wrong to want these things?** (Not necessarily. We all want to be liked, coordinated, good looking, etc. But when admiration turns to jealousy, problems arise. If someone who has a special gift of hospitality decides he or she wants to be a teacher instead, and stops being hospitable to others, then the "body" becomes weak.)

5. It's weird to think of a body as one huge eye or one huge ear (vs. 17), **but sometimes a church "body" can get almost that lopsided. In our own group, what "parts" do you think might be a little oversized? What parts would you consider underdeveloped?**

6. If God gave you great singing ability, would it be better to become a famous recording artist or to only sing in church for free? Should people make money by using their gifts? Why or why not?

7. Is it OK to say, "I'm a hangnail, so leave me alone"? Why not (vss. 27-31)? (Even as we develop and practice our own gifts, we are to "eagerly desire the greater gifts" [vs. 31].

Paul is preparing to launch into the "love chapter," and he makes it clear that no one is exempt from being a "giving" part of the body.)

8. **What keeps you from doing more with your spiritual gifts?** (Knowing what they are; lack of time; inability to get along with others; desire to have other gifts instead, etc.)

9. **If this group *were* a living body, how would you say our physical condition is—excellent, good, fair, or needing intensive care? Why?**

Say: **Paul never had the chance to compare the church to a sports car. But you do. Which of the following parts best describes the function you feel you play in the church or in our group? If you don't hear your part, tell us what yours might be.**

- **radio: keeps us singing**
- **shock absorber: makes it smoother for the other parts**
- **antenna: ready reception to God's voice**
- **spark plug: gets us fired up**
- **steering wheel: keeps us headed in the right direction**
- **spare tire: gets us back on the road after a blow out**
- **windshield: has a clear view of where we're going**
- **chrome: adds pizazz**

Discuss what kids' gifts might be. Then ask: **Is our group missing any parts? What's the maximum speed we could get this "car" up to?**

MOTOR CITY MISMATCH

rubber	door handles
stainless steel	windshield
painted	headlights
fiberglass	seats
glass	tires
14-gallon	glove compartment
chrome	airbag
leather	exhaust pipe
sparking	gas tank
carpeted	engine

I CORINTHIANS 13

All You Need Is Love

Though the church body contains many gifts (chapter 12), love is the quality that holds them all together. Most of our gifts are temporary, and will not be needed when we "see [God] face to face," but love will continue.

Get four volunteers to act out the skit on the reproducible sheet, "The Hate Boat." Then discuss: **Would you rather be surrounded by love or by hate? Why? How did the people in this skit express hate? Which do you think is easier to "catch" from someone else—love or hate? Why?** Explain that this chapter takes a detailed look at what real love looks like.

DATE I USED THIS SESSION _____ GROUP I USED IT WITH _____

NOTES FOR NEXT TIME _____

_____

_____

1. Make up your own quote by completing this sentence: "A life without love is like a _____ without a _____ ." (Examples: A new car without a key; a great meal without a plate; a house without a roof, etc.)

2. Do you know anyone (verses 1-3) who can speak in the language of angels? Who can understand all mysteries? Who has faith that moves mountains? Who has given everything to the poor? Who has been put to death for following Jesus? On a scale of 1 to 10 (10 highest), how much would you be impressed by each of these people if you knew them?

3. Do you know anyone who shows love? How impressed are you by that? (Compare to verses 1-3. Spiritual gifts are important, yet they are useless unless they are fueled by love.)

4. Give examples (either positive or negative) that you have personally witnessed of how love is:

- **patient**
- **kind**
- **protective**
- **forgiving (keeps no record of wrongs)**
- **trusting**
- **hopeful**
- **persevering**

5. Give examples (either positive or negative) that you have personally witnessed of how love is not:

- **envious**
- **boastful**
- **proud**
- **rude**
- **self-seeking**
- **easily angered**

6. Which of the qualities of love in this chapter would you look for in a person you were dating? Would other qualities be more important to you? Why or why not?

7. What's the connection between love and truth (vs. 6)? (Love rejoices in the truth. It can't be based on lies.) **What does this mean, in practical terms, when you say that you love your parents, or that you love your friends?** (It's more than a matter of telling people what they want to hear. Being honest is difficult. But half-truths don't add up to real love.)

8. **Do you think love is ever painful? Explain.** (When love is not returned, it certainly is. God's love for us resulted in the death of His Son. Love is often painful, yet we should never try to avoid pain by withholding love.)

9. **What things might be more important to some people than being loving?** (Power; wealth; sex; popularity or other surface substitutes for true love, etc.)

10. **Do you think people are more loving as children, or as adults?** (As we get older, it becomes harder to love because we are a lot less trusting of other people. But as we choose to show love, we probably express it at a stronger level. The more we leave behind the "childish" [selfish] aspects of love, the more authentic is our experience of love.)

11. **When it comes to being a Christian, what childish ways** (vs. 11) **have you put behind you? Which are you holding on to?**

It's easy to say, "I'm in love," or even, "I love my parents." Challenge kids to assess their "love lives" by examining one relationship in light of this chapter. Have each person list the characteristics listed in verses 4-7, then pick a relationship (boyfriend, girlfriend, parent, same-sex friend, etc.) and check off each quality he or she consistently shows in that relationship. (You might recommend this exercise for kids who are wondering if that "special someone" who pledges love really means it.) After kids have assessed their own expressions of love, have them go through the list again, writing ways in which God has shown that quality to them.

THE **HATE** BOAT

Characters: Lisa, Tim, Captain Stewing, Grumbler

LISA: Oh, Tim, I'm so excited. An ocean cruise! What a wonderful honeymoon!

TIM: And on the famous *Love Boat*, too! There's the captain. Let's go meet him before the ship gets underway.

LISA: Hi, captain. I'm Lisa, and this is Tim. We're—

CAPTAIN: Get lost, you punks. I've got a ship to run.

TIM: Get lost? That doesn't sound like the captain of the *Love Boat* to me!

CAPTAIN: *Love Boat?* This is the *Hate Boat*, you idiot. The *Love Boat* is at the next pier.

LISA: But we're supposed to be on the *Love Boat*. We've got to leave right away!

CAPTAIN: Too late, suckers. Step off this ship now and you're shark bait.

TIM: But we're on our honeymoon. We paid a lot for this trip!

CAPTAIN: So what? Now leave me alone. I have to go make some old people walk the plank. *(Exits)*

LISA: Tim, what are we going to do? I don't want to spend my honeymoon on something called the *Hate Boat*.

TIM: Hold on. There's a guy who looks like a waiter. Excuse me, sir!

GRUMBLER: Yeah, what is it?

TIM: Does this boat have beautiful cabins and a giant swimming pool, like the *Love Boat*?

GRUMBLER: Are you kidding? We got scuzzy cabins and a mud puddle.

LISA: But we love to swim!

GRUMBLER: Hey, if the ship starts leaking, maybe the puddle will get bigger.

TIM: Do you have huge banquets and live stage shows?

GRUMBLER: We got stale tuna fish sandwiches and a dead parakeet.

LISA: Tim, this is ridiculous! If you'd gotten your directions straight, we'd be on the *Love Boat* now!

TIM: If you hadn't been jabbering so much, maybe I could have heard the directions!

LISA: Is that right? Well, maybe you should have married somebody else!

TIM: Maybe I should have! Then neither of us would be on the *Hate Boat*!

GRUMBLER: So what's the problem? You two seem to be on the right boat to me!

I CORINTHIANS 14

Gifts with Strings Attached

Some spiritual gifts—particular those of prophecy and speaking in tongues—are often controversial. One thing, however, is clear: The public use of any spiritual gift should benefit the whole church, not just the one who has the gift.

(Needed: Someone who speaks a "foreign" language)

Find someone (student or adult) who is reasonably fluent in a language that most of your group members don't speak. Introduce this person and tell the group that he or she is a guest speaker and that everyone should listen closely to every word. Then have the person speak, but in the foreign language. The speaker should try to communicate with gestures and tones, but without deviating from the foreign language. Students who have studied the language may pick up some of what's being said. Others may be completely lost. Later, explain that speaking another language takes skill—yet the value is seen only when someone's around who understands. In this chapter, Paul will make similar observations about the gift of speaking in tongues.

DATE I USED THIS SESSION _____ GROUP I USED IT WITH _____

NOTES FOR NEXT TIME _____

_____

_____

1. Describe a time when you found it extremely difficult to communicate with someone. What made it so hard?

2. In this chapter, Paul deals with two spiritual gifts that both have to do with communication: prophecy and speaking in tongues. Based on verses 1-5, how would you describe the difference between them? (Prophecy is a message from God that the Holy Spirit communicates to a Christian. It may be what He wants the church to do, or a prediction of what will happen in the future. Speaking in tongues is the ability to speak in an earthly foreign language without ever being taught it [as the apostles did in Acts 2:1-12] or, as some believe, to speak a language of prayer and praise that people don't comprehend [unless God provides such ability to an interpreter] but that God understands. Churches disagree over whether and in what forms these gifts exist today; be ready to explain your church's perspective.)

3. What impact do you think speaking in tongues would have (or does have, if they've experienced this) on you? What impact do you think someone else's speaking in tongues would have on you? (Compare their responses to verses 6-12, where Paul notes that people with the gift felt special, yet it was only beneficial for them. In a church setting, no one else could understand what was being said. It was something like an orchestra warming up before the concert— the sounds were there, but in no meaningful arrangements. Perhaps some of your group members can relate to the responses of unbelievers as described in verses 22-25.)

4. What parts of worship besides speaking in tongues could verses 13-17 apply to? (In this case of speaking in tongues, Paul's concern was that even though the spirit of the believer was worshiping God, the mind wasn't necessarily on the same track. How many of us can say that we have never sung a hymn or recited a prayer while our minds were miles away?)

5. Do you think Paul is discouraging the use of certain spiritual gifts (vss. 18-21, 26-40)? (It may seem so, but he then makes it clear that he is only trying to ensure that they are used properly—to benefit the church.)

6. How do churches today try to maintain a sense of order? (Following an established procedure; bulletins to show the order of events, etc.)

7. Do you think our church needs to be more orderly, or do you think we need to "loosen up" a little? Explain.

8. Can you picture someone visiting our group, seeing what we do, and saying, "God is really among you!" (vs. 25)? Why or why not? How would our group need to change for something like that to happen?

9. Look at verses 33-35. How do you feel about this instruction? What is Paul's point? (The point, as in the rest of the chapter, is orderly worship. Apparently there was a problem with some of the Corinthian women interrupting services by asking questions. Most women in that culture received little education, and Paul wanted them to save their questions to ask their husbands at home. Some Christians believe this instruction was meant just for that time; others still apply it in their services today. Be ready to explain your church's position.)

Whether or not the gifts of prophecy and speaking in tongues are practiced at your church, kids can apply the principle Paul teaches here: Gifts and abilities are for building up the church, not just for our personal benefit. The reproducible sheet, "Use or Abuse?" helps kids apply that principle specifically to your group. After you've brainstormed ways that each ability could be used selfishly and unselfishly, ask: **How could you use one of your abilities to build up this group?**

If you get a great new CD for your birthday, you can listen to it by yourself and really enjoy it. You can also play it for your friends and let them enjoy it. You can even crank the volume way up so the neighbor down the street who's desperately trying to get her baby to sleep can enjoy it. After all, it's good to share your presents, right?

USE OR ABUSE?

For each of the "presents" (gifts or abilities) listed here, think of a way someone could use it unselfishly in our group–like sharing your CD with your friends–and a way to "share" it selfishly–so that people really wish you'd keep it to yourself! The first example will help you get started.

GOOD LISTENER
Use it: Be there for people who need someone to talk to
Abuse it: Gossip about the things people have told you

SENSE OF HUMOR
Use it:

Abuse it:

GOOD IDEAS
Use it:

Abuse it:

FRIENDLY/ OUTGOING
Use it:

Abuse it:

LEADERSHIP ABILITY
Use it:

Abuse it:

QUIET, GENTLE ATTITUDE
Use it:

Abuse it:

ABILITY TO ASK THOUGHT- PROVOKING QUESTIONS
Use it:

Abuse it:

CONCERN OVER HOW OTHERS ARE DOING
Use it:

Abuse it:

KNOWLEDGE OF THE BIBLE
Use it:

Abuse it:

Death Bites the Dust

Jesus' resurrection was the first of many bodily resurrections to come. The assurance of eternal life should motivate us; otherwise, we could just party through this life with no concern for anyone but ourselves. But Christ has conquered death, and believers share in His victory.

Play "Partner Tag." With an even number of players, designate one person to be "It." The person is supposed to tag someone who isn't touching a partner. It is up to the other group members to keep moving around the room and forming different pairs to prevent anyone from being tagged. Kids must change partners at least every 10 seconds. Anyone tagged without a partner becomes the new "It." Later, point out that as we face the future, death, and the resurrection, we have nothing to fear as long as we're "partnered" with Christ.

DATE I USED THIS SESSION _____ GROUP I USED IT WITH _____

NOTES FOR NEXT TIME _____

_____

_____

1. What was the last "Elvis sighting" you heard about? Why do you think people try to keep up the myth that Elvis Presley is alive?

2. When Jesus rose from the dead, some people understandably thought it was a hoax. But what difference between "Elvis sightings" and "Jesus sightings" helped people believe (vss. 1-8)? (Jesus didn't appear to a single lonely person at a gas station in the middle of nowhere. He made numerous appearances that could be verified—in one case, to more than five hundred people at once.)

3. But that was almost two thousand years ago. How is it that people come to believe in Jesus today? (Point students to verses 8-11. Just as Paul had a personal encounter with Jesus even after His ascension, so can we—though ours aren't usually quite so dramatic. As people saw the changes in Paul's life and the energy he put into carrying out his faith, people believed in Jesus. As people today see the changed lives of Christians, they may become less resistant to the call of Jesus in their own lives.)

4. Do you know people who believe that when we die, that's it —that we won't live eternally? Paul had the same experience. Even some of the best-educated religious leaders (the Sadducees) didn't believe in the resurrection. How would you respond to people like that? Compare your response to what Paul says in verses 12-29. What parts of his argument could you use to defend the resurrection if someone asked you about it?

5. Which phrase describes your life better: "I die every day [by making sacrifices for Christ]" or "Let us eat and drink, for tomorrow we die"? What does that say about how important the resurrection of the dead is to you (vss. 30-34)?

6. If we're going to be resurrected anyway, then why do we have to die (vss. 35-49)? (Death is the transformation from an imperfect human body to a perfect body adapted to the spiritual world, not unlike a wrinkled little seed being planted, dying, and becoming a full-sized plant in all its glory.)

7. How do you feel when you read verses 50-57? How do you suppose you would feel about them if someone close to you had just died?

8. Paul says that knowing we'll have life after death should motivate us to "stand firm" and believe that our faith in God and our work for Him is never wasted (vs. 58). If you take that view, what good could you see coming out of the following true story?

David (not his real name) went to a big youth rally one Saturday night. A speaker urged all the kids to wear a special piece of jewelry to school during the next week. It was a multicolored chain; each color stood for part of the "plan of salvation" (red for the blood of Jesus, gold for heaven, etc.). The idea was to get other kids asking about how to become Christians. Several of the Christian kids from David's school said they'd do it. But on Monday, David was the only one who did. He wore the chain all week, all by himself, feeling kind of stupid. A couple dozen kids asked him about the chain, and he explained the colors. Some kids laughed; some didn't. Not one said he or she wanted to become a Christian. Was David's effort wasted?

(Seeds and planter [optional])

The reproducible sheet, "Victory Song," gives kids a chance to express some of the strong emotions thoughts of death may evoke. You may be surprised at how effective this activity can be with even the most unlikely writers. When everyone is done, read the "poems" to the group (without naming the authors, if this makes kids more comfortable). If possible, consider having everyone plant some seeds in a window box or planter. As plants come up, they will be reminders of death, resurrection, and the expectation of better things to come.

How do you feel when you read about death? What do you think of when you remember Christ's big win over the grave? Share your thoughts by writing a poem—a song without music—addressed to Jesus. Use the letters of the word VICTORY to start each line. Here are some guidelines to help you, but don't get stuck on them if something else fits you better.

1st line: Write a line that expresses a visual image you get when you think about death or resurrection. (If you're stuck for V words, try Victory, Vanished, Voices, Visible, Vacant, Violent.)

2nd line: Express an emotion you feel about death or resurrection.

3rd line: Describe something Jesus does or will do.

4th line: Tell about one thing in your life today that is affected by the knowledge of future resurrection.

5th and 6th lines: Start over with a visual image or emotion if you like, or just go "free form."

7th line: Summarize the poem. (Stuck for Y words? Try You, Yes, Yesterday, Yell.)

Some general hints:
• DON'T try to make it rhyme!
• Write a line, not just a word for each letter.
• Consider breaking lines in interesting ways—in the middle of a sentence, for example.
• Borrow or modify a line from I Corinthians 15:50-58 (line 7 of the sample is taken from verse 54).

Sample:

Vacant graves?

I can't believe my eyes!

Can you really have brought those old bones back to life?

That makes me think there's hope for me!

Only God could raise the dead!

Retreat, Death—

You have been swallowed up in victory!

Now you try it:

V

I

C

T

O

R

Y

Put Your Money Where Your Mouth Is

As Paul closes his first letter to the Corinthians, he sends greetings to and from many of his personal friends and shares his plans for the future. He also passes along instructions regarding giving to the church and standing firm in the faith.

Have three volunteers act out the skit on the reproducible sheet, "Pledge Break." Ask: **Do you think God wants Christians to have more money than non-Christians have, the same amount, or less? Why?** Explain that Paul made no secret of the fact that Christians can expect to make financial sacrifices.

DATE I USED THIS SESSION _____ GROUP I USED IT WITH _____

NOTES FOR NEXT TIME _____

_____

_____

1. Some people accuse the church of always trying to get money from people. Why do you think they have that impression? Is it accurate?

2. What are three important reasons why churches need money? What's one way churches use money which doesn't seem too important to you? How much money do you think our youth group should spend in a year?

3. Do you feel that our church needs *your* money? Why or why not? Do you give regularly, as Paul suggests (vss. 1-4), or are you more likely to give for a one-time, special cause? (Paul wanted people to give regularly—even for special needs. [His concern was for the church in Jerusalem, which was facing famine and persecution. He encouraged the churches he visited to help out the Jerusalem Christians.] He preferred not to have to take special collections, even for gifts like this one.)

4. If we all gave a little more to our church than we do now, what new things do you think we could accomplish? (Focus both on how your own church could benefit, and how you could help provide for the needs of others.)

5. Would you be more willing to give to a cause if someone sent you a letter, or if someone asked you in person? Why? (Even though Paul was asking by letter, he did mention that he planned to drop by in person [vss. 5-9].)

6. If you'd just read the Book of I Corinthians as a letter, your head would probably be swimming with information by this point. So Paul was kind enough to summarize (vss. 13, 14) before he signed off (vss. 15-24). In what ways do you try to:

- be on your guard?
- stand firm in the faith?
- be men (or women) of courage?
- be strong (spiritually)?
- do everything in love?

7. In the last part of this letter, Paul mentions helpful Christians who "deserve recognition" (vs. 18). What could we do in this group to "recognize" people who do something special for the Lord?

Young people, perhaps more than any other age group, have a hard time making a priority of giving. They've only recently begun to earn money themselves, so they are keenly aware of how hard it is to get. They probably don't have much income, but anticipate significant expenses—not only for things they'd like to own, but often for college. Urging them to be consistent about giving for God's causes may not make you popular. But faithful stewardship is a mark of discipleship that needs to be cultivated even in the teen years. Spend some time sorting through the attitudes your group members have about giving. Ask questions like the following:

• **Do you think of your money as yours to do what you choose with, or as God's? How does your view affect your daily spending decisions?**

• **Why do you suppose giving seems so important to churches?** (Not only because they need the money for their ministry, but because it reflects a level of Christian maturity and gratitude to God.)

• **Do you think God expects you to give something even if you are saving for college or some other worthwhile expense?**

• **Are you pleased with how much and how regularly you give to Christian causes? Do you think God is pleased?**

• **How will you let God influence the way you spend and give money during the next month?**

PLEDGE BREAK

Characters: Telly Vangelist, Chris Chun, Announcer

(Telly Vangelist and Chris Chun are seated at a table facing the audience. Announcer is standing off to the side.)

Telly: And welcome to *Sixty Seconds of Power*, where the only rock is the Rock of Ages and the only roll is the one up yonder. I'm Telly Vangelist, and my guest today is Chris Chun—with a compelling testimony of how he found salvation and riches on the great highway of life. Mr. Chun, your story, please.

Chris: Uh, Telly, I'm afraid you've misread your notes. I didn't find riches, I found kitchens. I'm here to tell you about my ministry in the soup kitchens downtown.

Telly: Isn't that amazing! Finding riches in the soup kitchen! We'll hear more, right after this.

Announcer: You, too, can find fame, fortune, and a bad toupee if you act now! Operators are standing by to receive your pledges. Pledge one million dollars and Telly will pray for you right on the air! Pledge one thousand dollars and Telly will mention your name among the list of supporters at the close of our program. Pledge one hundred dollars and Telly will include your name when he is singing in the shower. Act now! Operators are standing by to take your call!

Telly: We're back with Chris Chun, who is going to tell us how he turned a soup kitchen into a multi-million-dollar franchise. Yes, friends, it pays to serve God. Chris?

Chris: But I didn't get rich serving God. In fact, it's cost me a lot—if we're just talking about money.

Telly *(clapping his hand over Chris' mouth)*: Whoops! We're experiencing technical difficulties. So we'll take a pledge break and hear how God will make you rich if you send in your pledges right now.

Announcer: That's right, Telly. This limited-time offer is almost too good to believe! Send us your whole year's income, and in just two months you'll receive three months' income! What a blessing! Some restrictions may apply.

Telly: Well, that's all we have time for today, folks. Join us next week, when we'll examine the question, "What kind of luxury car does God like best?"

II CORINTHIANS 1

Comfort Able

Having planned to visit the church in Corinth, Paul writes II Corinthians to explain why his plans have changed. He assures the readers that just as we share in "suffering" because of our faith in Jesus, we also share in the comfort He provides.

(Needed: Lifesavers, toothpicks, and bowls)

Divide the group into teams. Give each team one roll of Lifesavers and each person one toothpick. Have teams sit in rows, side-by-side, holding their toothpicks in their mouths. At your signal, see which team can be the first to have one person open the roll of Lifesavers, place one at a time on his or her toothpick, and pass each one down the line, toothpick to toothpick, until the last person drops it into a bowl at the end. Other than the first person, no player may use hands at any time. If anyone uses hands or drops a Lifesaver, it goes back to the beginning of the line. (If it breaks, one is taken from the bowl.) The first team to successfully transfer all its Lifesavers from the roll to the bowl is the winner. Later, point out that we should transfer more important things—such as comfort—from one person to another.

DATE I USED THIS SESSION _____ GROUP I USED IT WITH _____

NOTES FOR NEXT TIME _____

_____

_____

1. Has anyone ever come to you for comfort? Were you able to help? Why or why not?

2. Have you ever needed comforting, but couldn't seem to ask anyone for it? Why do you think it was so hard to ask?

3. How could you comfort each of the following: (a) a crying baby; (b) a six-year-old brother or sister who lost a favorite toy; (c) a friend whose parents are getting a divorce?

4. We may tend to think of God more in terms of discipline than comfort. What are some things He expects from us that may not be exactly comfortable? (Denying self; taking up our "cross"; turning the other cheek when wronged; loving enemies, etc.)

5. How do "the sufferings of Christ flow over into our lives" (vs. 5)? (People demanded Christ's crucifixion because He had offended them by speaking the truth. If we stand with Him and speak the truth, too, we're likely to attract persecution, too.) **Do you think that you'll suffer less or more for being a Christian in the future than you have in the past? Why?**

6. How have you felt comforted by the Lord when you were going through a hard time (vss. 1-7)? Did the help come directly from God, through reading the Bible, through another person, or in some other way?

7. Have you ever been under so much pressure that you weren't sure you could stand it (compare vs. 8)? How did you make it through? Have you ever felt the way Paul describes—that you couldn't count on yourself, but only God could get you through (vss. 8-11)?

8. Apparently some of Paul's enemies were claiming that Paul was unreliable because he'd said he'd visit Corinth—and his plans changed. From reading verses 12-17, do you get the feeling that Paul had made promises he never intended to keep? (Paul emphasizes that he made his plans with sincerity.)

9. Paul writes that even though he couldn't follow through on his plans, we can be sure that God will follow through on His promises (vss. 18-20). **What "yes"es had the Corinthians experienced from God (vss. 21, 22)?** (He helped them to stand firm, marked them as His, and gave them His Spirit.) **How has God said "Yes" to you?**

10. **If you were buying clothes, what brand names would you look for? If you were going to a movie, whose reviews would you trust? If you were buying something bigger like a car or electronics, what "seals of approval" might you look for? Why?** (Seals of approval acknowledge established levels of quality, and brand names give us certain expectations, or perhaps reflect some degree of status. Similarly, Christians carry God's "seal of ownership" [vss. 21, 22]).

11. **How do we know God will honor all the promises He has made to us (vss. 22, 23)?** (He has given us the Holy Spirit "as a deposit," so we are able to see that He does indeed have the power to do what He says.)

12. **Which of God's promises mean the most to you? Why?**

The reproducible sheet, "Don't Hog the Covers," will have group members list the things through which they find comfort. When they finish, compile a master list. Then discuss: **Which of these are things we receive from God? Which ones should we pass on to other people so they'll experience more comfort? Which ones have side effects that might not be good for us? Which ones have the most effect on you when you're feeling bad? Why?** Challenge kids to make this more than a mental exercise—to actually carry out their "comfort plans" during the week.

DON'T HOG THE COVERS

To some people, a "comforter" is a blanket or quilt that keeps them warm—sort of like the one you see here. But real comfort comes from many sources. On each of the squares of this comforter, draw or write something that provides comfort for you when you're feeling depressed, worried, or generally lousy. We've started the quilt for you; fill in as many of the other squares as you can. If the examples we've given don't apply to you, just cross them out.

	A NOTE FROM A FRIEND		
			(pie)
(personal stereo)			
		READING THE PSALMS	

Now think of one person who could use some comfort this week. What two or three things from your comforter could you share with this person? Then don't just pull the covers over your head and leave your friend out in the cold—be a comforter!

"Praise be to the God and Father of our Lord Jesus Christ, the Father of compassion and the God of all comfort, who comforts us in all our troubles, so that we can comfort those in any trouble with the comfort we ourselves have received from God" (II Corinthians 1:3, 4).

What Stinks?

Paul assures the Corinthians that, though he may have expressed some strong opinions and changed his plans, he by no means meant to cause them confusion or grief. He also reminds them (and us) that all believers are to be "the aroma of Christ."

(Needed: Assortment of "smelly" things and covers for them)

Have a quiz based on smells. Provide a variety of items that should be identifiable by their scents—either pleasant or foul. Bring some assorted foods (peanut butter and coffee are said to be most identifiable), window cleaner, crayons, moth balls, etc. Be sure kids can't see what they are smelling. (It will probably be easier to cover the items than to blindfold the whole group.) See who can identify the most scents, and credit him or her as being "The Group Member Who Smells Best." Ask: **Does God have a sense of smell?** Then hold that thought until you discuss verses 14-16.

DATE I USED THIS SESSION _____ GROUP I USED IT WITH _____

NOTES FOR NEXT TIME _____

_____

_____

1. Have you ever had to visit someone you didn't want to see? What was the visit like?

2. It wasn't that Paul didn't want to visit with the Corinthians—he did! But he knew that to visit them would be "painful." Why? (See verses 1-4. Paul had written them previously, telling them some things they probably didn't want to hear. They would have to discuss the problems when he came in person, which wouldn't be easy on either Paul or the Corinthians.)

3. If you love someone, do you think you should overlook all of his or her faults, and not be "picky"? Why do you think Paul wrote to confront the Corinthians about things that caused him "great distress and anguish of heart"? (Genuine love is based on truth. If the Corinthians were doing things that could have harmed them, Paul had to be completely open with them. Besides, he had the responsibility to oversee their spiritual growth. We can overlook the shortcomings of others, but we shouldn't ignore sin. It's far better to find a loving, helpful way to put them back "on the right track.")

4. Would you ignore the following problems, or try to do something about them? Why? If you chose to do something, what would you do?

• Your boyfriend or girlfriend chews with his or her mouth open, which really bothers you.

• Your younger brother has started hanging around with kids who are rumored to use drugs.

• A friend, depressed about getting cut from the football team, makes a half-joking remark about suicide.

5. Confrontation is intended to lead a person to feel sorry and want to change. Once that happens, those involved ought to forgive him or her (vss. 5-11). Reading between the lines, do you think the Corinthians were bigger on punishment or forgiveness? (It seems that someone had been expelled from the fellowship of the church for a time.

[Perhaps this was the one mentioned in I Corinthians 5, though many do not believe so.] That punishment had apparently done the job it was intended to—led him to repentance—and now the church needed to stop punishing and start forgiving.)

6. **Based on verses 12 and 13, do you think God has in mind just one place that you should be at any given minute? Why or why not?** (Not necessarily. There may be more than one good place we could be, more than one good thing we could be doing. Paul went to Troas and had an "open door" to preach, yet was not at peace—so he went elsewhere.)

7. **Look at verses 14-16. In what way do Christians "smell"** (vss. 14-16)**?** (Just as a hungry person can be drawn to the kitchen by a turkey roasting in the oven, spiritually hungry people are attracted to the "fragrance" of a personal relationship with Jesus. And to God, His people should have the "aroma" of Jesus. Of course, to people who reject Jesus and face eternal death, Christians are "the smell of death.") **How good would you say you smell to God? Is your "scent" strong enough to attract other people to want to be Christians?**

8. **What do you expect to get in return for serving God?** (Compare answers with verse 17. While we receive many benefits because of His grace, we should never take God's gifts for granted. We should serve out of sincerity rather than for any kind of profit.)

Use the reproducible sheet, "You Smell Terrific!" to draw out some practical ways in which kids can be "the aroma of Christ." After they've filled in some ideas individually, discuss how they can act on their suggestions in everyday life.

YOU **SMELL** TERRIFIC!

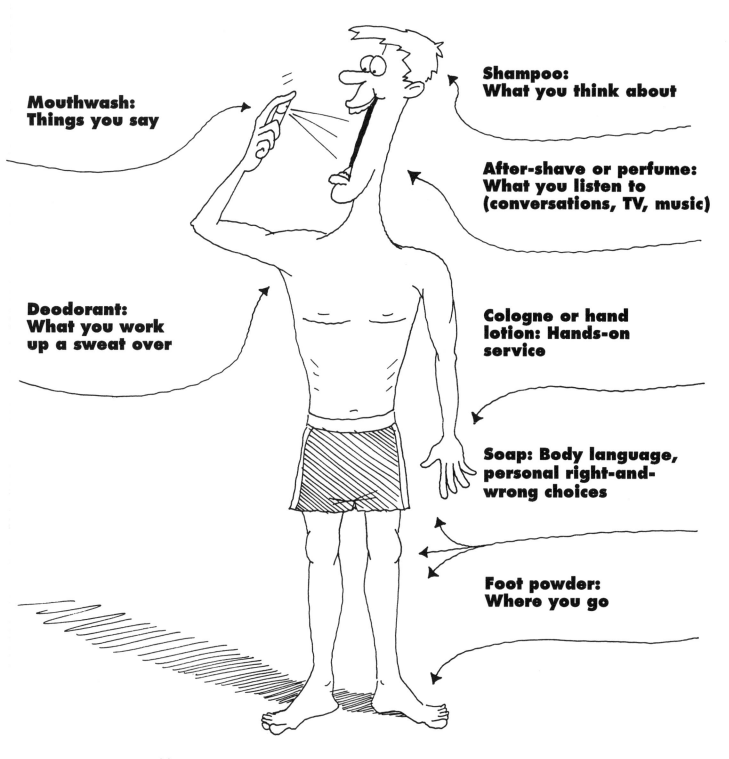

**Mouthwash:
Things you say**

**Shampoo:
What you think about**

**After-shave or perfume:
What you listen to
(conversations, TV, music)**

**Deodorant:
What you work
up a sweat over**

**Cologne or hand
lotion: Hands-on
service**

**Soap: Body language,
personal right-and-
wrong choices**

**Foot powder:
Where you go**

How is your personal hygiene? Does what you say, where you go, and what's important to you send a fragrance that's pleasing to God and attractive to others? Or do you . . . well . . . reek? For each area labeled, list one or two specific things you can do to be sure your "smell" pleases God and attracts others to Him.

II CORINTHIANS 3

The Transformer

Paul appeals for his readers to trust his motives. Because of God's new covenant, we can now be led by the Holy Spirit rather than driven by strict adherence to a set of laws. And we can be "transformed into His likeness with ever-increasing glory."

(Needed: Prize [optional])

Cut apart a copy of the reproducible sheet, "All Talk, No Action," and hand each command to a volunteer. Explain that each must describe his or her activity in one minute without using any gestures and without saying the forbidden words on the sheet. (You may even want to tie volunteers' hands behind their backs.) Let the group vote on who did the best job, and award a prize if you like. This should lead in to a couple of points from this chapter: Paul's defense of himself based on his actions (to refute those who would twist his words), and the difference between the written law and the living example of the Holy Spirit.

DATE I USED THIS SESSION _____ GROUP I USED IT WITH _____

NOTES FOR NEXT TIME _____

_____

_____

1. Have you ever asked someone to write a letter of recommendation for a job interview or college application? If you needed such a letter, what would you want it to say?

2. When you're trying to get a job or get into college, how important are letters of recommendation? Why? (Though many organizations require them, people are almost never hired solely because of someone else's letter. The personal interview must match what is said in the letter, or the recruiter/boss will be suspicious.)

3. Why did Paul bring up letters of recommendation at the start of this chapter? (He was pointing out his authority as an apostle. Some lesser-known teachers needed such letters. And traveling phonies who claimed apostolic authority sometimes falsified such letters for themselves.)

4. Paul didn't need letters of recommendation as he traveled from place to place. Instead, he considered the changed lives of people his "letters" (vss. 1-3). What people might be able to point to you as evidence of their teaching and ministry? Are you the kind of "letter" they can be proud of?

5. If you told someone how to become a Christian, or helped someone through a difficult time, how much credit would it be right for you to take? Why? (Compare to Paul's comments. Such activity was the goal of his life, and he found great joy in the spiritual development of other people. Yet he never forgot to give God the credit for making the change in other people [vss. 4-6].)

6. What does Paul mean that "the letter [of the law] kills, but the Spirit gives life" (vs. 6)? Does this mean that it's not important to obey the written laws of God? (Not at all. However, the Law has limitations in its ability to bring people closer to God. Those who try to earn their own salvation by obeying the Law will fail. But belief in Jesus through the work of the Holy Spirit gives us life.)

7. In the Old Testament, the evidence that Moses had been in the presence of God was a radiance that shone from his head. He even had to wear a veil while around other people (Exodus 34:29-35). **But now we can relate to God directly, "unveiled"** (vss. 7-18). **How have you experienced that direct relationship?** (Possibilities: Through prayer; a sense of closeness; an assurance of forgiveness, etc.) **How would you like to?**

8. **Do you ever feel as if there's a "veil" between you and God? Between you and understanding the Bible? Between you and the people you wish would become Christians? Explain.** (Point out that having these "veils" doesn't necessarily mean we haven't become Christians ourselves. Verse 16 refers to the ability of many Jewish people to understand how Christ has fulfilled the laws of Moses. The Holy Spirit can take our "veils" away, the more we understand His work in our lives and seek to follow His leading.)

9. **How could your relationship with God make you personally "very bold"** (vs. 12)? **If you were ten times as bold as you are now, what kinds of things would you do for God this week?**

10. **What evidence can you give that you "are being transformed into His likeness"? If you can't think of any, what do you suppose that means?**

Continue to contrast the letter of the law with the new, personal life through the Spirit. Discuss: **Has your relationship with God grown as much as your friendships have during the same period of time? Explain. How would you like God to "free" you? Do you offer others the freedom to be open and honest with you without "biting their heads off"? How are you more in the "likeness" of God now than you were a year ago? How do you expect to be more like Him a year from now?**

All Talk, NO ACTION

Explain how to tie a shoe without using any gestures or using the words

- SHOE
- TIE
- LACE
- FOOT

Explain how to brush your teeth without using any gestures or using the words

- TEETH (or tooth)
- BRUSH
- TOOTHPASTE
- MOUTH

Explain how to kiss without using any gestures or using the words

- LIPS
- MOUTH
- PUCKER
- KISS

Explain how to blow your nose without using any gestures or using the words

- NOSE
- BLOW
- TISSUE (or any brand name of tissue)
- HANDKERCHIEF

II CORINTHIANS 4

Impermanent Press

Though the message of the Gospel is a "light," Satan has blinded some people to the truth it presents. Christians who carry this treasure do so in "jars of clay," showing that salvation comes through God's power, not our own. Even though we may be persecuted, we can stay confident that He will see us through.

(Needed: Three shoe boxes, one brick)

Invite three volunteers to compete in a strength contest. See how quickly the first volunteer can flatten an empty shoe box. See how quickly the second volunteer can do the same. But the third contestant will have a brick (or some other unflattenable object) in his or her shoe box (since you secretly placed it there before the session). After the contest, explain that this chapter talks about being hard pressed but not crushed—because of the treasure of God in us.

DATE I USED THIS SESSION _____ GROUP I USED IT WITH _____

NOTES FOR NEXT TIME_____

_____

_____

1. What percent of people would you say are completely honest—with no lies, deceit, half-truths, flattery, cheating, stealing, covering up for other people, etc.?

2. Why is the truth so important in our relationships with other people (vss. 1, 2)? (If we lie about other things, how can people trust what we say about Jesus?)

3. Have you ever talked to a non-Christian about God or church or the Bible, only to have the person laugh at you or otherwise reject you? How did you feel? If some people don't seem able to believe what we tell them about God, does that mean we said the wrong things to them (vss. 3, 4)? (Sometimes, but not necessarily. People who continue to reject God and follow their own sinful desires don't have the spiritual "eyes" to recognize the light of the Gospel. They're blinded by "the god of this age.")

4. In discussing the Gospel with others, we're supposed to be servants (vss. 5, 6). How do you feel about playing such a lowly role? Why? (One good thing about being a servant is that you don't have to have vast knowledge or great persuasive skills—and you don't have to hit a certain percentage of "successes." We simply tell others about Jesus and leave the rest to God. We should do all we can to "make His light shine [out of] our hearts," but we aren't responsible for those who choose to ignore it.)

5. Where do you keep your most valuable possessions? How do you protect them?

6. God places His "treasure" in some pretty plain-looking, not-so strong containers: us (vs. 7). Can you give some examples of people who have done more for God than you would expect from looking at them? What have you done for the Lord that you could not have done on your own?

7. What would you say is the worst thing that could happen to you because you are a Christian? (Some people die for their beliefs [but don't let group members off with such an "easy" answer]. The situations they must *live* through—rejection, persecution, confusion, etc.—probably will cause them more pain in real life.)

8. Why doesn't God keep us from trials like these (vss. 8-12)? (If people knew nothing bad would ever happen to them, they would turn to Christianity out of purely selfish reasons. It takes no faith to sidestep pain and problems. But faith and perseverance grow as we see God stand by us while we go through the trials of life.)

9. If death and life are both at work in you (vs. 12), which do you think is winning? Why?

10. What's the worst thing you faced last week? What would it take for you to consider such things as "light and momentary troubles" (vss. 13-18)? (Focusing on "eternal glory" can help our perspective.)

11. What keeps you from taking a long-term view of your troubles? What makes you forget that God is going to see you through even the worst of times? (Examples: Hanging around the wrong people; infrequent church involvements; lack of staying close to God, etc.)

When we're truly hard pressed (vs. 8), it can be hard to claim God's promises. Help group members share their needs by using the reproducible sheet, "Share Your Struggles." When everyone has had a chance to complete the sheet privately, allow volunteers to share their requests. If your group is not ready for this level of openness, collect the sheets (let kids cross out any requests they don't want read, even anonymously) and read them to the group without revealing names. Then pray together. Urge group members to continue praying for each other on their own. Be available to talk later with kids who are especially stressed by pressures, questions, people, and struggles.

Share Your STRUGGLES

Life throws some pretty tough problems at us. Parents divorce. Friends drop us cold. School is too much for us. We try and try and try to resist a temptation but finally fall flat into sin. We feel ashamed. We feel defeated. We feel alone.

Do you need God to hang on to you right now? Do you need other people to hang on to you? Share some of the reasons here. These sentence-starters can help you put your struggles into words.

I AM "HARD PRESSED" BECAUSE OF THESE PRESSURES:

Needing money for_____.

Fighting with _____.

Having trouble in_____ class.

All the _____ in my neighborhood.

All the _____ at home.

Not having enough time to_____.

Feeling like I have to_____.

Other:_____.

I AM "PERPLEXED" BECAUSE I DON'T HAVE ANSWERS TO THESE QUESTIONS:

Why would God let _____?

What will happen when _____?

Why doesn't God _____?

Why am I_____?

When will I get to _____?

Other: _____?

I AM "PERSECUTED" BY THESE PEOPLE:

A teacher:_____.

A school administrator:_____.

Another student: _____.

A parent: _____.

A brother or sister: _____.

Another relative:_____.

Someone in this group: _____.

Other: _____.

I AM "STRUCK DOWN" BY THESE STRUGGLES:

Being tempted to _____.

Not being able to find _____.

Always having to_____.

Never getting to_____.

Missing _____.

Wishing I were_____.

Other: _____.

II CORINTHIANS 5

Diplomatic Community

We are ambassadors of Christ. As we mature spiritually, we want to be closer to God, but are limited by our human bodies. Yet someday we will stand before Him, so we should prepare for the day of judgment and live as His "new creations."

(Needed: Name tags; refreshments)

Before the session, write the names of various countries on name tags, one country per tag (enough so that each group member will have a tag). Select countries that are involved with each other—some as allies, some as enemies. When the meeting starts, set out refreshments and give each person a tag. Announce: **You are all ambassadors at the United Nations. You represent the nation named on your tag. Your job is to represent your country in the best possible light.** Have kids mill around, conversing "in character" for several minutes as they eat the refreshments. Set up some potential confrontations by introducing ambassadors of enemy countries to each other. Later, as you discuss the concept of being "Christ's ambassadors," draw parallels from this activity.

DATE I USED THIS SESSION _____ GROUP I USED IT WITH _____

NOTES FOR NEXT TIME _____

_____

_____

1. Do you have any stories of not-so-great camping trips that you can share? Why is camping out such a challenge sometimes? (Discuss being away from the "comforts" we're accustomed to, and being exposed to threatening elements—possibly without the training we need to face such things.)

2. How is being a Christian like camping out (vss. 1-4)? (When we become Christians, we discover a spiritual world where we truly belong—with a loving Father, a new body, and a Savior who is preparing "mansions in heaven" for us. But for now we are stuck in a very imperfect "tent" [our human body].)

3. How do you suppose the Holy Spirit is our "deposit," guaranteeing better things to come (vs. 5)? (As we sense His presence in our lives, we can be convinced of the reality of everything else God has promised.)

4. How do you "live by faith, not by sight" (vss. 6-9)? What invisible things do you wish you could see?

5. What reasons might each of the following Christians have for wanting to be "away from the body and at home with the Lord": (a) a man serving a life sentence in prison; (b) a 15-year-old girl who has to use a wheelchair; (c) a 16-year-old guy who has no more problems than anyone else does? How could each of these people apply verse 9?

6. If we're saved by faith and not by works, how do you explain the judgment Paul talks about in verse 10? (This judgment will not determine our salvation—Christ already took care of that. But it will be a time to give account of how well our lives expressed our gratitude for that salvation.)

7. What might be the most persuasive thing you could say to another person about believing in Christ (vs. 11)? What might be the most persuasive thing you could do? How much time would you say you spend in a typical month trying to persuade people to believe in Christ?

8. How might people consider Christians "out of their minds" (vss. 12, 13) when they talk about God? How do you feel about that possibility? When you look at Paul's motivation (vss. 14, 15), do you feel any braver about sharing your faith?

9. A Christian is supposed to be "a new creation" in which "the old has gone, the new has come" (vss. 16, 17). As we make this transition, what are some of the "old" things we tend to hang on to? What are some of the "new" things we have a hard time doing?

10. If we've received Christ, we actually belong with Him in heaven—and some day we'll be there. But for now, we have the assignment of serving as His ambassadors (vss. 18-21). **What "rights" might an ambassador have to give up in order to represent his or her country in the best light?** (The right to wear or say or do whatever he or she feels like; the right to reject commands from superiors, etc.) **How could you be a better ambassador in the future than you have been?**

11. Why might some people resist being "reconciled to God" (vs. 20)? As ambassadors, what should we do when others don't respond as we want them to? (We should remain calm and open to "renegotiation" at a later time. Our job is to keep speaking and acting in ways that honor God. The Holy Spirit will take care of the results.)

The reproducible sheet, "What Next?" develops the concept of becoming a "new creation." When group members finish, discuss as much as they're willing. (Some possible answers to Part I: [1] an explosion; [2] dinosaur skeleton or oil; [3] grape juice or raisins; [4] an older child or a wet diaper; [5] melted ice cream or a weight gain.) After talking about answers to Part II, emphasize that it can take time for our behavior to catch up with our "newness." Ask kids to share progress they've made in these areas. Have them pray silently about their continued growth.

WHAT NEXT?

Part I
If each of these items is step one, what's the next step?
Draw what "happens" next in each case.

1.

2.

3.

4.

5.

Part II
Now do the same thing with yourself. If you belong to God, what kind of "new creation" is He turning you into? What do you hope is "next" for you in each of the following areas?

The way you react when somebody puts you down

Your relationship with your father

The image that comes to mind when you think of what God is like

Your relationship with your mother

What interests you most about the opposite sex

Your relationship with your brothers and/or sisters

The way you feel about church

Your confidence around other people

What you tend to do when you're depressed

Your attitude toward poor people

What you tend to think about when you're bored

Your attitude toward rich people

Your ability to really enjoy life

"If anyone is in Christ, he is a new creation; the old has gone, the new has come!"   (II Corinthians 5:17)

II CORINTHIANS 6

No Yoking Matter

Living a faithful Christian life isn't always easy, but it's always rewarding. We should appreciate God's grace, serve Him in spite of the circumstances we face, and try not to cause others to stumble in their spiritual development. And we should beware of bonding with unbelievers because the difference in priorities will be sure to cause problems.

(Needed: Cord or rope)

Have kids compete in a three-legged race. Match up some kids of similar size—and some of very different sizes, if possible. After the races, ask: **Were the teams fair?** Point out that unevenly matched partners often have a tougher time; this chapter will discuss unequally matched partners in life.

DATE I USED THIS SESSION _____ GROUP I USED IT WITH _____

NOTES FOR NEXT TIME _____

_____

_____

1. What kinds of presents can you pretty much count on getting each year? On which holidays are you sure to get presents? What people can be counted on to send you gifts? How does all this affect your attitude toward the presents you get?

2. How do people take God's grace (His free, undeserved gift of salvation) for granted (vss. 1, 2)? (Christians can forget how much they need forgiving, or the terrible price Christ paid for their salvation. Some nonbelievers sense God calling them but keep putting off making a decision. When it comes to salvation, says Paul, now is the day.)

3. Do you ever complain about how hard certain parts of your life are? If so, which ones? Do you think your sufferings are worse than those of other people? Explain.

4. Do you think your life is harder, or easier, because you're a Christian? Why?

5. Paul had a lot to say about his hardships in verses 3-10. Do you think he was whining? Explain. (Instead of whining, he was showing how hard he had tried not to do anything to cause others to "stumble" spiritually.)

6. When you think about being a Christian, do you think about things like troubles, hardships, distress, and hard work? Why or why not? Paul listed as many positive experiences as he did negative ones. Which of these have you experienced (vss. 6-10)?

7. What can we learn from Paul about showing affection to others (vss. 11-13)? (Many of the Corinthians didn't like Paul, yet he did nothing to hold back his appreciation for them. Our kindness toward others should not depend on their responses.)

8. What do you think it means to be "yoked together" with someone (vs. 14)? (Discuss the farm practice of yoking two animals side-by-side to work together in pulling a plow or vehicle.)

9. What problems might occur if a Christian is "yoked" to a non-Christian (vss. 14-18) **in the following situations?**

- **Partners starting a new business**
- **Marriage**
- **Dating**
- **Best friends**

10. Have you known of any Christians "yoked" to non-Christians, whose different priorities caused problems for them? What happened?

11. If you went on a TV talk show and said, "Christians should only marry Christians," what do you think the audience's reaction would be? If a non-Christian of the opposite sex wanted to "get serious" with you, what would you tell him or her?

(Needed: Coins)

The simulation game on the reproducible sheet, "The Yoke's on You," may help kids see the tensions between not being "unequally yoked" and still being an influence in the world. Make enough copies of the game board so that no more than four or five kids are playing together. Kids should flip a coin to see how many spaces to move (one space for heads, two for tails). Use coins for game pieces, too. As kids play, prompt discussion on the decisions they face and the consequences that result.

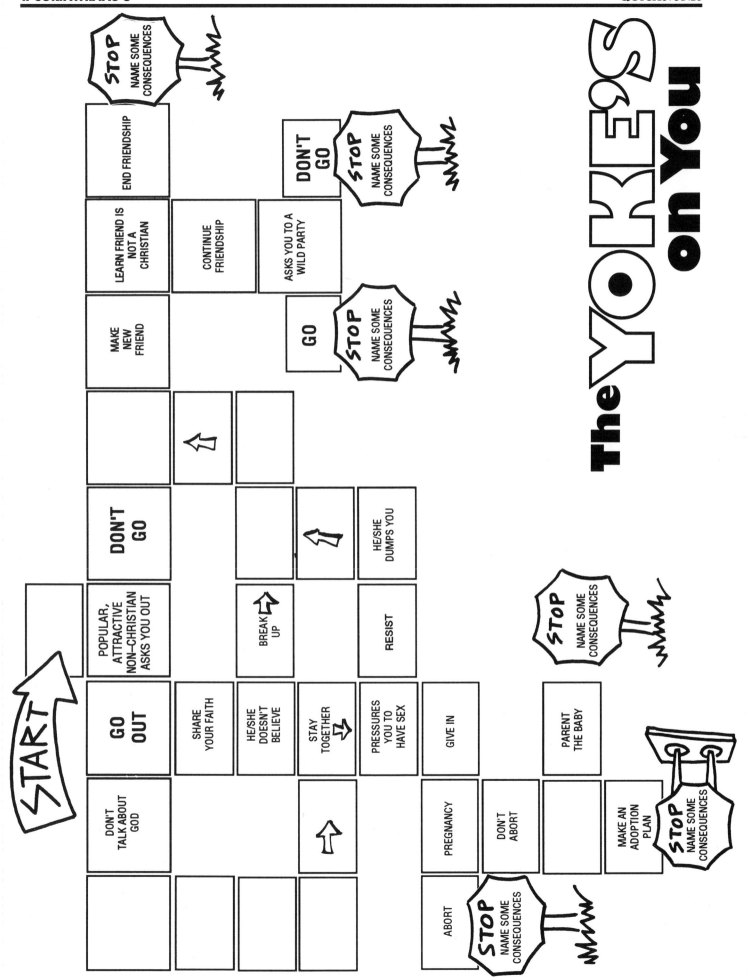

II CORINTHIANS 7

A Sorry Story

In a personal section to the Corinthian Christians, Paul expresses joy for their spiritual growth and maturity. He had previously written a "painful" letter to address a serious problem in the church, and the Corinthians had responded positively.

Before the session, copy and cut two sets of cards from the reproducible sheet, "Categories." When the session starts, form two teams. Each team must choose a "clue giver." Give each team's clue giver a copy of the first card. The clue giver must then call out clues (items that fall into that category) to his or her team, which must guess the category. The team to guess the category first (set a limit of 30-60 seconds) wins that round. Use different clue givers in each round. Save the categories, "Things That Harm Our Bodies," "Things That People Take Pride In," "Things That Make People Sad," and "Things That Make People Happy" for last; use them to lead into the themes of this chapter.

DATE I USED THIS SESSION _____ GROUP I USED IT WITH _____

NOTES FOR NEXT TIME_____

_____

_____

1. How can two imperfect people form "perfect" friendships? Do you think it's because the people involved don't know about each other's shortcomings; because they ignore each other's faults; or because they try to help each other overcome weaknessness? Why?

2. Based on Paul's comments, what do you think of his relationship with the Corinthians (vss. 1-4)? (He had confidence and pride in them.)

3. Yet Paul had previously written a letter to the Corinthians that he felt might hurt them. Have you ever said anything to someone that made the other person cry (out of sorrow, rather than joy)? How did you feel? Why?

4. Put yourself in Paul's place. You really love these people, but it's been a while since you've seen them in person. You get a report that they're involved in something that can harm them, so you write a hard-hitting letter and send it. How would you feel as you waited for a reply? (Tense; worried about being rejected, etc.)

5. How would you have felt when you got the report from Corinth, delivered by Titus (vss. 5-7)? (Paul must have been greatly relieved to know that the Corinthians still respected him and regretted their previous actions.)

6. If you had to tell a friend that something he or she was involved in could hurt spiritually, what would you do? How could you tell the truth without driving the person away? (We can't control how the person responds, but we're instructed to speak the truth in *love* [Ephesians 4:15]. People know when we're truly concerned about them, not just trying to "get on their case.")

7. What's the difference between "godly sorrow" and "worldly sorrow" (vss. 8-10)? Can you give an example of each one? (Godly sorrow is regret that we've sinned against God or another person; it leads to forgiveness and a clear conscience. Worldly sorrow is often just regret over getting caught.)

8. If you've done something wrong and feel bad, how can you tell if your sorrow is "godly" or "worldly" (vs. 11)? (Godly sorrow is marked by wanting to be forgiven; alarm over the wrongness of what you've done; desire for right to win out, etc.)

9. How did the Corinthians know Paul really hadn't given up on them after he wrote his letter (vss. 12-16)? (Paul had told Titus what a good group of people the Corinthians were, and then Titus showed up in Corinth.) **Who has stuck with you in spite of your shortcomings? Who have you refused to give up on even though that person has made some mistakes or even sinned against you?**

10. Can you give an example of each of the following?

* **Things that contaminate the body and spirit** (vs. 1)
* **Things that refresh the spirit** (vs. 13)

Ask group members to recall all the things they've been sorry for recently, and to evaluate which ones involved godly sorrow and which involved worldly sorrow. Discuss: **Are there some things in your life you ought to apologize (to God or to another person) for? Do you think people say "I'm sorry" often enough? Why do you think some people find it so hard to apologize for anything? How do you feel when others just seem to expect you to overlook their rudeness, making no effort to apologize or even admit that they may have hurt you? Other than with words, how can you show someone that you're sorry?**

CATEGORIES

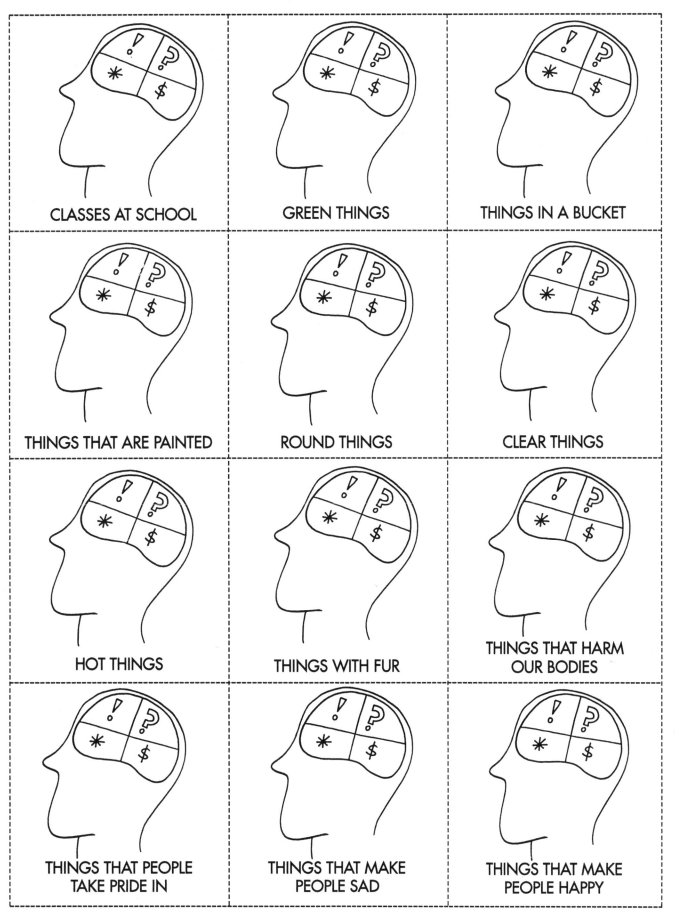

CLASSES AT SCHOOL

GREEN THINGS

THINGS IN A BUCKET

THINGS THAT ARE PAINTED

ROUND THINGS

CLEAR THINGS

HOT THINGS

THINGS WITH FUR

THINGS THAT HARM
OUR BODIES

THINGS THAT PEOPLE
TAKE PRIDE IN

THINGS THAT MAKE
PEOPLE SAD

THINGS THAT MAKE
PEOPLE HAPPY

II CORINTHIANS 8

Pennies from Heaven?

Paul cites the generosity of the Macedonian church as an example of how voluntary giving can be a sign of real faith and concern for others. Paul urges the Corinthians toward a greater degree of sharing. If we give to others when we are able, Paul writes, they may well do the same when we are the ones in need.

(Needed: Ten pennies for each group member)

Give each group member ten pennies (or ten of some other item) and these instructions: **Your goal is to get rid of all your pennies. You may give them away only one at a time. If someone tries to give you a penny, you must accept it. The person with the fewest pennies when I call, "Time," is the winner.** After a few minutes of frenzied trading, see how things have turned out. Then point out that Paul makes the surprising statement that when you try to give away your money you may end up getting just as much.

DATE I USED THIS SESSION _____ GROUP I USED IT WITH _____

NOTES FOR NEXT TIME _____

_____

_____

1. Have you ever given something away, even though you really could have used it yourself? What motivated your decision to do so (or not do so)?

2. Are these true of you or not?

• I would give more to others if I had more myself.

• I sometimes hesitate to give because I don't know much about the people or organizations who ask me.

• I don't know many people who need money more than I do.

• If I really wanted to, I could spend a lot less on myself and find another use for the money.

3. What was the last good example of giving that you witnessed? (Acts of unselfish giving may motivate us to reconsider our own attitudes.)

4. Have you ever believed in a cause so strongly that you volunteered to give, rather than waiting for someone to ask you? How do you think Paul felt when the Macedonian churches volunteered their money (vss. 1-5)?

5. When the Corinthians were doing so well in other areas like faith, speech, knowledge, earnestness, and love (vs. 7), was it fair of Paul to tell them they had to be better givers, too? Do you have some spiritual strengths that you hope "balance out" your weaknesses? Explain.

6. How do you feel you measure up when you compare your giving to what you know of what others give? To that of Jesus (vss. 8, 9)?

7. When Paul suggests we compare ourselves with others, he doesn't necessarily mean to compare amounts, but willingness based on what you have (vss. 10-15). How "acceptable" (vs. 12) would you say your level of giving is?

8. Have you seen examples of people giving to others and later being helped out when they were in need (vss. 13-15)? Do you think it spoils your motives if you think someone might return the favor someday? Explain. (Taking care of each other is part of being Christians. It may not be your main motive for giving, but it can provide some of the security you need to give generously.)

9. Think of some organizations that ask people for money. Which do you trust? Which don't you trust? Why? Would you have felt comfortable with the way Paul handled fundraising (vss. 16-24)? (He recruited Titus and a couple of other trustworthy people to take care of the money and make sure it was properly administered.)

Divide the group into two teams. Give each team one half of the reproducible sheet, "Enough to Go Around." Put each team in separate parts of the room. Each team is to figure out how to accomplish its ministry goals. Eventually someone may get the idea of combining resources with the other ministry. Reread verses 13-15 and discuss: **What keeps us from applying these verses? How might churches have a bigger effect if we were more willing to share with each other? How can we apply this idea to our group? How could a closer relationship with other Christians at school help you make more of a difference there?**

Enough to Go Around

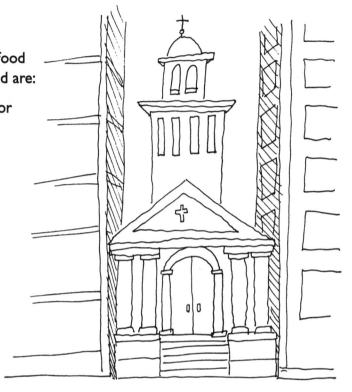

FIRST URBAN CHURCH

You help the homeless in your community through a food pantry, a thrift shop, and a shelter. Resources you need are:

- $500 worth of used clothing and household goods for the thrift shop
- $500 worth of canned goods and staples for the food pantry
- 20 cots for the shelter
- buildings for all three ministries
- 10 volunteers to staff the ministries

Divide up the resources you have to accomplish your ministry:

- 30 people
- a building with 4 rooms
- 20 cots
- $500

FIRST SUBURBAN CAMPUS MINISTRY

You help high school students by providing leadership training and summer outreach trips. Resources you need are:

- 25 leaders (volunteer or paid at $100 each)
- a building for a student-run outreach ministry to the poor
- transportation to outreach ministry fields (10 buses or $2,000 for travel expense)

Divide up the resources you have to accomplish your ministry:

- Five people
- Five buses
- $250 worth of food
- $250 worth of clothes and household items
- $1,000

II CORINTHIANS 9

Attitudes of Gratitude

Giving is like farming: The more that is "sown," the greater the potential of the harvest. When gifts are both given and received with proper gratitude, God is glorified through the process.

(Needed: Rope)

Let kids have a tug of war. Then explain that some people give their money the way the losing team gave up its rope: grudgingly and only under pressure.

DATE I USED THIS SESSION _____ GROUP I USED IT WITH _____

NOTES FOR NEXT TIME _____

_____

_____

1. When you hear someone describe how great a certain person is, do you always believe what you hear? Why or why not?

2. Paul had been telling one church (the Macedonians) how good another church (the Corinthians) was at giving (vss. 1-5). Now some representatives of the first church were likely to visit the second. If you were Paul, what would be your concern? (Paul knew the Corinthians had promised a generous gift, but they were still in the process of collecting it [8:11, 12]. Paul wanted to give credit where it was due, but he wanted to make sure he wasn't overstating the commitment of the Corinthian church.)

3. Do you know anyone you would classify as a "grudging giver" (vs. 5)? Do you like to ask this person for favors, loans, etc.? Why or why not?

4. According to Paul, the more you give, the more you experience the benefit of giving (vs. 6). Have you found this to be true yourself? Do you know anyone who has? Explain.

5. On a scale of 1 (stingy) to 10 (very generous), how do you give to the following: (a) the church; (b) your family's needs; (c) Christian organizations other than the local church; (d) people who just don't have enough (due to a house fire, illness, tornado, etc.)?

6. Why would someone give to church or the needy out of a sense of duty (vs. 7), not because he or she really wants to? Why not refuse to give at all instead? How do you think people develop this attitude? (Some think they can earn their way to heaven; others feel guilty for having so much, etc.)

7. Do you know people you would consider "cheerful givers" (vs. 7)? How do you think people develop that attitude? (The person must take greater joy in the work being accomplished with the money than in the money itself. Many of us tend to focus more on what the money can do for us, rather than for God or for other people.)

8. Is Paul saying in verses 8-11 that giving to God's work is a good way to get rich? Explain. (God provides for those who continually pass His blessings on to others. That kind of person is "rich" in a way that many wealthy people will never know. But the point of God's blessings is so that we can pass them on, not keep them.)

9. When someone is generous to you, do you thank God as well as the person (vss. 12-15)? Why or why not?

10. How have you benefited from God's "indescribable gift" (vs. 15) to us? (Jesus is truly a gift that keeps on giving. His supply of love, comfort, peace, etc., is never ending. While much of the rest of the world seeks fulfillment in cash reserves, possessions, etc., we should continually seek to be closer to Him as we remember that "every good and perfect gift is from above" [James 1:17].)

The idea of giving sounds noble and rewarding. But it's hard to part with our hard-earned money. The reproducible sheet, "Cheerfulness Test," will challenge kids to think about how cheerful they are during various "giving" opportunities. When they finish, explain that our attitudes toward giving reflect deeper attitudes toward money. While we should be wise in our spending, saving, and investing, we should also be cheerful in our giving. Then ask some questions that will get to the heart of your students' true feelings about money:

• **If you were carrying your life savings and were mugged, and you had an 80 percent chance to disarm the mugger and escape safely, would you still hand over your money, or would you resist?**

• **If a close family member lost his or her uninsured house to a tornado and needed all the money you have saved, would you let him or her have it to rebuild? What if the same thing happened to your best friend? To a casual acquaintance?**

• **Do you think anyone thinks you're selfish? Why?**

Cheerfulness Test

- You know how hard it is to get money.
- You sweat for it by mowing yards and having paper routes.
- You suffer the shattered eardrums and bruised shins of baby-sitting.
- You take minimum-wage jobs that no one else would have (slinging burgers, mopping floors, etc.).
- The begging skills you use on your parents would be envied by the street people of Calcutta.
- After long weeks and months (and perhaps years) of work, you finally get a little saved up.
- Then, lo and behold, other people come along and want you to shovel some of it in their direction. In each of the following cases, circle the expression that best reflects your attitude (or create one of your own).

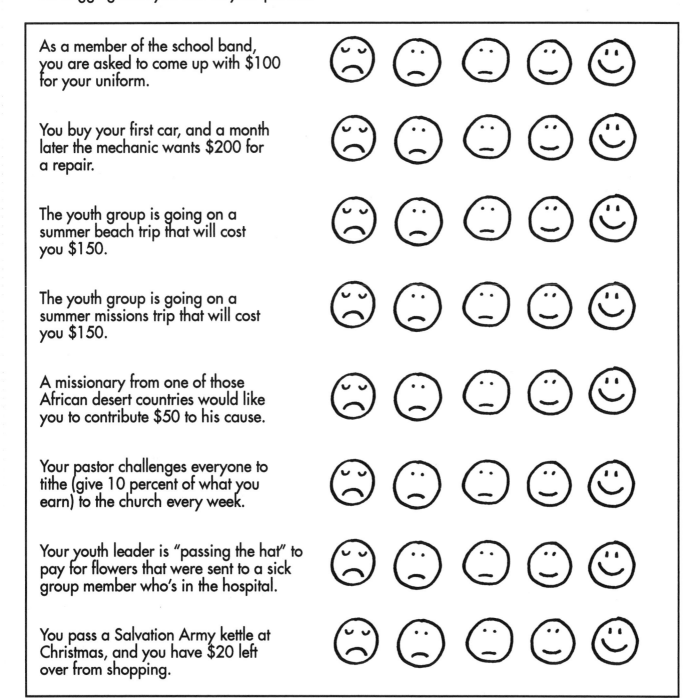

As a member of the school band, you are asked to come up with $100 for your uniform.

You buy your first car, and a month later the mechanic wants $200 for a repair.

The youth group is going on a summer beach trip that will cost you $150.

The youth group is going on a summer missions trip that will cost you $150.

A missionary from one of those African desert countries would like you to contribute $50 to his cause.

Your pastor challenges everyone to tithe (give 10 percent of what you earn) to the church every week.

Your youth leader is "passing the hat" to pay for flowers that were sent to a sick group member who's in the hospital.

You pass a Salvation Army kettle at Christmas, and you have $20 left over from shopping.

II CORINTHIANS 10

Braggers Anonymous

Paul defends his ministry. He urges us to build up one another, not ourselves. If we're going to boast about anything, he says, we should boast about God.

(Needed: Masking tape)

Divide into teams of four to six people. Give teams five minutes to see which team can put a piece of masking tape highest on the wall, using only team members (no chairs, etc.) to climb on. For safety's sake, allow a human tower of no more than three. (If your group is too small to divide into teams, have the group compete against its own best mark.) Explain that in this chapter Paul addresses people who were trying to build themselves up to be greater than anyone else.

DATE I USED THIS SESSION _____ GROUP I USED IT WITH _____

NOTES FOR NEXT TIME _____

_____

_____

1. When are you more open and honest with other people—when you're writing them a letter, or when you're talking to them face-to-face? Why? (Some kids may avoid the "unknown" elements of personal confrontation and prefer composing their thoughts on paper. A few may be too sensitive to say something in a letter that they wouldn't say in person.)

2. Paul didn't always have an option. He divided his time among a lot of churches, and he spent several years in prison—so personal contact wasn't always possible for him. He had been accused of being "timid" in person and "bold" in his letters. Do you think he agreed (vss. 1, 2)? (To a small extent this might have been true, yet Paul never shied away from bold honesty whether in person or in responding by letter to accusations leveled against him.)

3. In the battle to make your own thoughts obedient to Christ (vss. 3-6), are you winning? Holding steady? Losing? Trying to "make a deal" with the other side? What's the hardest part of this battle for you?

4. Have you known anyone who thought he or she was better than most of the other Christians in the world—more committed, obedient, etc.? Why do some people develop this attitude? (Paul faced such people [vss. 7-11]. Some believers may look back at the way they were before becoming Christians, see how far they've come, and be amazed. Unfortunately, they can start puffing up with pride about how humble they are! But as we continue to mature, we can learn to stop looking back, and rather look ahead and see how far we still have to go.)

5. What are the things in life that you're proudest of? Might your interest in these things, and your comments about them, give anyone the idea that you're bragging? How can you prevent this from happening?

6. Are you more likely to spend time comparing yourself to others or focusing on the great things God has done (vss. 12-18)? How can you feel good about yourself, yet be modest? (We should "boast in the Lord." We should consider the things we do for Him worthwhile, because everything else pales in comparison.)

7. **For what things can you "boast in the Lord" today?** (Let group members share things God has done for them lately—and things they have done for Him.)

8. **Do you usually feel "commended" by the Lord (vs. 18)? Or do you tend to think that He's displeased with you? Where do you think you've gotten these ideas?**

(Needed: Rap accompaniment)

Give kids some practice in boasting about the Lord. The reproducible sheet, "Righteous Rap," uses a medium known for its bragging—but brags about the Lord instead of the rapper. Let kids come up with the three fill-in stanzas in small groups or individually. (The first stanza should list some amazing things God has made; the second should mention the benefits all Christians get from Christ's death and resurrection; the third should list specific things God has done for those writing the rap.) Then have kids perform their raps for each other.

RIGHTEOUS RAP

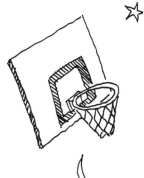

So you think you're really something? You think you're real hot?
Let me tell you of the awesome God I've got.
He was there before the start, before the beginning,
When he set the stars shining and the planets spinning.

He made . . .

But we humans went wrong, we really messed up;
So God sent His Son to drink our bitter cup.
His only Son, Jesus, was broken like bread,
But then the Father raised Him from the dead.

Because of that, we . . .

And that's why, when it's time to boast,
I think of what the Lord has done the most
Instead of bragging on the things I do,
I give the credit where credit's due!

For me He's . . .

II CORINTHIANS 11

Barefaced Faith

Faced with accusations by false teachers (whom he sarcastically refers to as "super-apostles"), Paul feels compelled to remind the Corinthians of the extent of his own ministry and sufferings. Though he feels such self-directed writing is "foolishness," he cares intensely for the Corinthians and knows they are being misled. He warns them against deceivers who masquerade as believers.

Form two teams. Seat the first team in a circle of chairs. Have a person from the second team stand behind each chair. Then you stand behind an empty chair and "lure" a seated person to your empty chair by winking at him or her. The person you wink at must try to leave his or her chair before the person directly behind grabs his or her shoulders. The first team gets a point for each escape; the second gets a point for each thwarted escape attempt. After the game, explain that Paul was dealing with people who were trying to lure the Corinthians away from Paul and his teachings.

DATE I USED THIS SESSION _____ GROUP I USED IT WITH _____

NOTES FOR NEXT TIME_____

_____

_____

1. Do you like to talk about yourself? In a group of people, how willing are you to open up about your likes, dislikes, and problems?

2. Paul didn't like to talk about himself. He called it "foolishness" (vs. 1). But he did it anyway in this case because he was so worried about what the Corinthians were hearing (vss. 1-6). What are some "different spirits" or "different gospels" which attract people today? (Reincarnation; teaching that Jesus was really married and had kids; that miracles can all be explained away, etc.)

3. When you come up against people who think they know a lot more about God than you do, how do you react? (Some people are good at using big words, and can cleverly twist the truth. Like Paul, however, each Christian has personal experience with God that can't be disputed. We should hold to the certainty of our relationships with God as we check out the validity of what others teach.)

4. When you listen to someone present a point of view—in a sermon, in a TV commercial, in a school assembly—how much are you influenced (on a scale of 1 to 10, with 10 highest) by the following: (a) the speaker's clothes; (b) his or her hair style; (c) smoothness of the presentation; (d) the number of jokes and stories? (Note that Paul's approach to spreading the Gospel involved servanthood and self-sacrifice. He didn't charge for his services. In contrast, the "super-apostles" probably looked pretty sharp [vss. 7-12]. But while Paul could do what they were doing, he knew they couldn't [or wouldn't] do what he was doing.)

5. These false teachers were "masquerading" as apostles (vss. 13-15). What kinds of masks do people wear in church these days? What are they trying to hide?

6. Paul mockingly says that since the Corinthians were putting up with these other foolish people, then they could tolerate his own "foolishness" for a moment (vss. 16-20). Then he launches into an incredible account of his exploits. Read verses 21-33, and suppose it's your turn to explain how much you've suffered for your faith. What

would you say? (No doubt Paul's opponents came up just as short as most of us do.)

7. **Is talking about yourself always the same as bragging? Explain.** (No. The more Paul spoke of his life, the more God was glorified. We can all "boast of the things that show my weakness" [vs. 30]. People know our shortcomings. Yet as we weather storms we couldn't possibly handle on our own, others will see God at work in our lives. And as we become more willing to talk about our feelings and experiences, He can be glorified.)

8. **If you made a movie about the "adventures" Paul lists in this chapter** (vss. 23-33)**, what would the title be? Who would you want to play the part of Paul? Why?**

The reproducible sheet, "Behind the Mask," will challenge kids to evaluate unbiblical messages that hind behind masks of acceptability. After giving kids time to work on these, have them share results. (Drawings may vary widely, but you're generally looking for physical evidence of anxiety, ruined health, disappointment, bitterness, etc.) Ask: **What other deceptive ideas are attracting kids you know? How could you help them see what's behind masks like these?**

BEHIND THE

M A S K

Some pretty rotten ideas are wearing some pretty good-looking masks these days. In the spaces provided, draw the kinds of faces that you think might be behind these masks. In other words, what might a person *really* look like after following each of these philosophies?

"Have sex with as many people as you can."

"Party till you puke!"

"Whoever dies with the most toys wins."

"Life is just a bad joke, so don't take anything seriously!"

"Shop till you drop!"

"Do unto others before they do unto you."

"Winning is everything!"

"The human mind can solve any problem."

II CORINTHIANS 12

Quit Sticking Me!

Christians are not spared pain as they go through life. Paul, who was privileged to get a "preview" of heaven, was still given a "thorn" to live with. The same God who assures us of eternal life stands beside us through all the frailties of our human condition.

(Needed: Tape or pins)

Before the session, cut the slips from a copy of the reproducible sheet, "A Thorn in My Back." As kids come in, tape or pin a slip to each person's back. By asking only "yes" or "no" questions of other group members, each person should try to guess what his or her "problem" is. After all kids have guessed their problems (or five minutes have passed), discuss: **How would it change your life if you *always* had the problem that was written on your slip of paper?** Note that Paul talks about his chronic "thorn in the flesh" in this chapter.

DATE I USED THIS SESSION _____ GROUP I USED IT WITH _____

NOTES FOR NEXT TIME_____

_____

_____

1. What's the most indescribable thing you've ever seen, tasted, or heard? Why would you single it out?

2. For the past several chapters of Corinthians, Paul has been responding to the accusations of a few false teachers who were trying to discredit him. Now he tells a story that he had kept to himself for 14 years (vss. 1-6). There's little doubt that Paul is talking about himself here, so why wouldn't he just say so? (Using the third person puts the emphasis more on what God did than on what happened to Paul.)

3. What's the "third heaven" (vs. 2)? Does this mean there are different levels of heaven depending on how "good" you are? (No. This probably refers to the place we usually think of as heaven—where God's throne is, and where believers will worship Him. The "first" heaven could be the earth's atmosphere, and the second could be outer space [which is why people sometimes refer to the sky and outer space as "the heavens."])

4. Why do you think Paul waited until this point to bring up the story? Why not use it as an opener to every sermon in a new town? (Perhaps because it would tend to raise more questions than answers. If Paul is not allowed to tell what he heard, it would only raise curiosity. But it is a powerful testimony to the authority of Paul's apostleship, which some people were questioning.)

5. How do you suppose Paul's "thorn in the flesh" kept him from developing an inflated ego (vss. 7, 8)? (He was reminded that he was ordinary flesh and blood like everybody else. [People speculate that his problem might have been vision problems, migraine headaches, epilepsy, or a speech disability.] And he learned that he didn't have a "pipeline" for getting what he wanted.)

6. Based on this, would you say God always answers our prayers (vss. 8, 9)? (Not in the way we wish. Sometimes His answer to our requests is no, because He knows of something that's better for us.)

7. How might people see God's power working in your life (vss. 9, 10) if you had the following "weaknesses" and relied on Him: (a) deafness; (b) fear of talking in front of a group; (c) a tendency to eat too much; (d) having to wear braces on your teeth?

8. Have you learned to "delight" in weaknesses, insults, hardships, persecutions, and difficulties? If so, in what ways? If not, do you think it's really possible? (These experiences are, on a spiritual level, what push-ups, weightlifting, and other exercises are on a physical level. They may cause a little sweat, soreness, and discomfort, but in the long run they make us stronger.)

9. Paul hadn't wanted to "toot his own horn" so much, and he was somewhat annoyed that he'd had to convince the Corinthians of his sincerity and spiritual authority (vss. 11-13). But he was planning to visit Corinth and wanted to be clear on what God expected of the Christians there (vss. 14-18). If he visited our group, how much of what he was worried about at Corinth (vss. 19-21) do you think he would find here?

Kids face their own "thorns," too. Distribute sheets of paper. Say: **Do you have something that keeps poking you, bothering you, never quite leaving your mind? Think honestly about that thing you wish you could change but that's out of your control. Is it the size of your nose? A learning disability? A relationship that causes problems? Write it down, using just enough specifics for someone to understand what you're bothered by.** Tell kids that others will see their answers, but that the writers will be anonymous. Then collect the sheets, redistribute them at random, and have each person write a "prescription" for dealing with the problem, based on Paul's experience. Encourage kids to be sensitive to the sufferers and careful to follow what the Bible says. Lend assistance where needed. If you have time, discuss the sheets, allowing writers to remain anonymous. Leave the sheets where the owners can collect them later. Challenge kids: **During the next week, how can you count on God's grace to be enough for you? How can His power be "made perfect" in your weaknesses?**

A THORN
IN MY BACK

OUCH!

I have a canker sore in my mouth.

I have a splinter in my thumb.

I have headaches all the time.

I have a toothache.

My nose is always stuffed up.

My hair is falling out.

I have a boil on my neck.

I'm allergic to cats and dogs.

I can't eat sugar.

I can't see without my glasses.

I have a cramp in my leg.

I can't talk louder than a whisper.

I can't sleep at night.

I have an ulcer in my stomach.

I can't stand loud noises.

Mid-Terms

As Paul ends his letter, he challenges us to test ourselves regularly to ensure that we're staying faithful. Our goal is perfection; so no matter how well we do, we can always set our objectives a little higher.

(Needed: Small objects to pass)

Have group members sit in a circle with one person in the center. While the center person closes his or her eyes, the people in the circle pass around an object (ring, coin, pen, etc.). When the center person says "Stop," whoever is holding the object is "It." Then the center person selects a letter of the alphabet and says "Go." At that point, "It" hands off the object and tries to name five things that *end* with the designated letter before the object makes its way around the circle. (Example: If the letter is "r," the words "hair," "screwdriver," "oar," "star," and "gear" would work.) If "It" succeeds, the center person tries again. If not, "It" goes to the center. This activity involves time limits and acting under pressure—two challenges to the Corinthians in this chapter.

DATE I USED THIS SESSION _____ GROUP I USED IT WITH _____

NOTES FOR NEXT TIME _____

_____

_____

1. **How do you usually feel before exams? How do you feel after?** (It probably depends on how well you think you did.)

2. **Paul warned the Corinthians that he would visit soon, and if they didn't deal with their spiritual problems on their own, he would give them a "spiritual exam" when he arrived** (vss. 3, 4). **If Paul gave this warning to our group, how would you feel?** (Prepared; needing to cram; offended by the idea of a spiritual exam, etc.)

3. **Paul suggests that the best way to be ready for this exam is to test ourselves right now** (vs. 5). **What do you think we should be looking for?** (Evidence of Jesus in our lives.) **How do we "pass" such a test?** (We will see that we are growing spiritually and becoming more Christlike as we apply what we hear.)

4. **What should you do if you fail the test** (vs. 5)? (Ask yourself whether you have really received Christ and are seeking to live for Him. If the answer is no, turn from your sins and receive Him.)

5. **It seems to be important to Paul to help the people pass this exam—not for his reputation as a teacher, but for their sake** (vss. 6-8). **What spiritual teachers are trying to prepare you for this exam? Do you usually welcome their "drilling" or resent it? Why?**

6. **Do you think Paul is setting an unrealistic goal for us** (vss. 9, 11)? **Explain.** (Our goal is perfection. We will reach this goal only after we die, but God has begun the process already in this life. Our job is to set our sights on the goal and not resist God's work in our lives.)

7. **Is it pointless to have a goal we know we will never reach? Explain.** (Young people may have weight-loss or financial goals they don't truly expect to reach, yet they don't stop trying to be thinner and richer. Similarly, the closer we get to perfection, the more satisfied we will be.)

8. Which of the following do you think would be the best place to put your faith to the test: (a) on a summer mission trip to Central America; (b) living in the inner city; (c) living in the suburbs or a small town; (d) living in a rural area; (e) just going to school; (f) in your home? Why? What could you learn about your faith in each of these places?

The reproducible sheet, "Do-It-Yourself Test," will help kids examine themselves for some indicators of Christian growth. Because kids are creating their own tests, there will be variations from student to student. Don't worry about this; what's important is that kids recognize the Bible as the measuring standard—and get some experience drawing principles from it for themselves. You may want to spend some time discussing other possible passages that would be useful for self-testing. As kids suggest criteria, challenge them to demonstrate that those criteria are biblical to ensure that they aren't making false assumptions about what's expected of maturing believers.

DO-IT-YOURSELF
T E S T

Don't you just hate tests? Well, that's usually because someone else puts it together to show you how much you don't know. This time *you* get to write the test. We're told to test ourselves to see whether we're continuing to grow as Christians. Fill in some specific qualities from the passages listed (use as many or as few as you think are important). Then test yourself.

I see this quality in my life . . .

	Never	Seldom	Sometimes	Often

1. Galatians 5:22, 23

2. I Corinthians 13:7

3. Matthew 5:3-11

Now make up a "25 words or less" essay question about your spiritual growth—and answer it.

GALATIANS 1

Fact or Fiction?

After hearing and at first responding to the Gospel, some people end up pursuing other religious ideas. This is a major problem in Galatia, where an organized group (the Judaizers) is trying to set up a much more legalistic system of religion. Paul writes to appeal for the faithfulness of the believers. And he begins by recounting his personal encounter with the living, powerful Lord.

(Needed: "Supermarket tabloid" newspaper)

Form two teams. Give each team half of a sensationalist "supermarket tabloid" newspaper (screen it first to make sure it's appropriate for kids to see). Each team should make a list of three headlines from its part of the newspaper—plus a made-up one of its own. The first team reads its four-headline list to the other team; the second team tries to guess which headline is made up. Then the second team tries to fool the first. Continue until you run out of headlines. Then explain that this chapter deals with telling fact from fiction.

DATE I USED THIS SESSION _____ GROUP I USED IT WITH _____

NOTES FOR NEXT TIME _____

_____

_____

1. What would you say are the three best things about your life? What are the three worst things?

2. Would you say the world we live in is basically good, or basically evil? Explain. Do you think it's gotten better or worse during the past 2,000 years? (As Paul began his letter to the Galatians, he referred to "the present evil age " [vss. 1-5]. We might describe our own time in the same way.)

3. Do you know of people for whom Christianity was only a phase—who seemed to get serious about Jesus for a while, but then moved on to some other interest? If so, why do you think they didn't stick it out? (Possibilities: Not a genuine commitment to begin with; not sufficiently rooted in scriptural truth; wanted the benefits, but unwilling to undergo spiritual discipline, etc.)

4. False teachers in Galatia were twisting the truth, and new believers were being fooled into following them (vss. 6-9). What kinds of false "good news" do people try to get you to believe today? (You can have all the sex you want as long as it's "safe"; you don't need forgiveness, because right and wrong are just a personal choice; you'll never get old or die; you can get drunk as long as you don't drive, etc.)

5. Do you work harder at pleasing people or at pleasing God (vs. 10)? Can you do both? (Many qualities that please God (love, joy, peace, etc.) also tend to please people. But other things that please God [standing for the truth, sharing your faith, etc.] make many people angry. So if we try to be people pleasers, we're in danger of displeasing Jesus. We must determine to obey Him even if that displeases others.)

6. Do you know anyone with a dramatic conversion story like Paul's (vss. 11-17)? If so, tell us about it. (Point out that Paul had been one of the primary opponents of Christianity—until Jesus dealt with him on a person-to-person basis. Paul had learned the truth about Jesus from the risen Lord Himself. So he knew what he was talking about, and he knew the teachers in Galatia were perverting the true Gospel.)

7. Have you ever wished the story of how you received Christ (if you have) were more dramatic than it is? Why or why not?

8. How can people who haven't experienced a dramatic conversion like Paul's be sure of the Gospel? (The Holy Spirit is given to all believers, not just those with great "testimonies." He will lead us into the truth.)

9. The Christian churches praised God when they heard about the changes in Paul's life (vss. 18-24). What changes in your life show others that God is working in you? What changes need to happen yet?

10. Do you think most everybody falls away from grace at one time or another? Explain. Why do you think Paul was so concerned about the ones in Galatia? (They were being actively misled. It's one thing to stumble during the growing process, but quite another to have someone continue to teach falsehoods that are contrary to the Gospel.)

Kids may think they could never fall for false teachings. They may wonder how anyone could even think of joining a cult or non-Christian religion. Have them consider the teachings on the reproducible sheet, "Yeah, That Sounds Good." When they finish, discuss their reactions. Pay special attention to any "I wish it were true" expressions; for example, many Christians wish everyone would ultimately be saved, but the Bible doesn't support that idea. Point out that this is how some people "fall" for cults—because they hear what they want to hear. You may want to have available a handbook that summarizes basic doctrines of various cults and other religions. Plan to follow up on unanswered questions in future meetings.

YEAH ----→ THAT SOUNDS GOOD

After each of the following teachings,
circle the words that best describe your reaction.

1 The idea of "past lives"—coming back over and over again as different people (reincarnation)

Sounds Great! •••• **Worth Checking Into** •••• **I Wish It Were True, but I Doubt It** •••• **No Way!**

2 The idea that God will not punish anyone in hell—that in the end, everybody will be saved (universalism)

Sounds Great! •••• **Worth Checking Into** •••• **I Wish It Were True, but I Doubt It** •••• **No Way!**

3 The promise of power to get sexual pleasure and control over others (Satanism)

Sounds Great! •••• **Worth Checking Into** •••• **I Wish It Were True, but I Doubt It** •••• **No Way!**

4 The idea of combining the "best" of many different religions (Baha'i faith)

Sounds Great! •••• **Worth Checking Into** •••• **I Wish It Were True, but I Doubt It** •••• **No Way!**

5 The idea that humankind is gradually improving until we will all reach perfection (Theosophy)

Sounds Great! •••• **Worth Checking Into** •••• **I Wish It Were True, but I Doubt It** •••• **No Way!**

6 The promise of eventually becoming a god (Mormonism)

Sounds Great! •••• **Worth Checking Into** •••• **I Wish It Were True, but I Doubt It** •••• **No Way!**

7 The promise of no more suffering and merging into "oneness" with God (Buddhism)

Sounds Great! •••• **Worth Checking Into** •••• **I Wish It Were True, but I Doubt It** •••• **No Way!**

8 The idea of fighting to defend your faith (Islam)

Sounds Great! •••• **Worth Checking Into** •••• **I Wish It Were True, but I Doubt It** •••• **No Way!**

9 The idea of changing the world by concentrating your thoughts with those of others in a "harmonic convergence" (New Age movement)

Sounds Great! •••• **Worth Checking Into** •••• **I Wish It Were True, but I Doubt It** •••• **No Way!**

10 The practice of not killing any animals—not even cattle that would be used for food (Hinduism)

Sounds Great! •••• **Worth Checking Into** •••• **I Wish It Were True, but I Doubt It** •••• **No Way!**

11 The idea that sickness and death are illusions that should be dealt with spiritually, not medically (Christian Science)

Sounds Great! •••• **Worth Checking Into** •••• **I Wish It Were True, but I Doubt It** •••• **No Way!**

12 The idea that we should follow principles set down by an ancient race of aliens from another planet (Scientology)

Sounds Great! •••• **Worth Checking Into** •••• **I Wish It Were True, but I Doubt It** •••• **No Way!**

GALATIANS 2

Peter and Paul Not Merry

Freedom in Christ is threatened when others try to add requirements for Christianity (in this case, circumcision) beyond placing faith in Him. Observing a strict set of rules won't create righteousness. Even Christians may try to add such requirements; when that happens, confrontation may be necessary.

Choose one or two people to be "outsiders"; have the rest of the group form a tight circle. The outsiders should try to force their way in, while those in the circle try to keep them out. Ask: **How did it feel to be outsiders? How did it feel to be forcing the outsiders to stay out?** Explain that Paul had to confront church leaders who were trying to keep new believers out unless they would conform to certain unnecessary standards.

DATE I USED THIS SESSION _____ GROUP I USED IT WITH _____

NOTES FOR NEXT TIME _____

_____

_____

1. What would you think of a church that decided whether or not people could join based on their physical appearance? Have you heard of any churches that do this? (Some churches still discriminate racially; the problem in this chapter was over a physical symbol of following Jewish law.)

2. As the first-century church began to grow, the believers faced this very situation. Some of the Jews (in this case it was a group referred to as Judaizers) believed in Jesus, yet because of many years of Jewish tradition they felt circumcision should also be a requirement (vss. 1-5). Why do you think this issue became such a big deal? Why not say, "Hey, see here, you Gentiles, you're getting heaven and eternal life out of this, so just go get circumcised"? (If one group of people added the requirement of circumcision, how many other groups might want to add more? Paul didn't want the church to emphasize externals over the heart [vs. 6].)

3. If you wanted to know whether someone was a "real" Christian, what outward signs would you look for? Would it be right to do that? Why or why not?

4. When Paul first carried the Gospel to the Gentiles (non-Jewish people), the only special instruction the other apostles gave was to remember to take care of the poor (vss. 6-10). How would you have felt if you were Paul and suddenly you discovered that the rules had changed?

5. Have you ever been criticized or "chewed out" in front of your friends by a parent, teacher, or some other authority figure? Did you deserve it? How did you feel? Do you think the other person enjoyed "making a scene"? Explain.

6. Paul found himself in a face-to-face, public confrontation with Peter (vss. 11-14). **Do you think Paul was wrong to do this? Why?** (Peter's actions had even misled Barnabas—to this point one of the most conscientious of the church leaders. In this case, public confrontation not only showed the offending apostles the error of their ways, but also acknowledged to the Gentiles present that they had been mistreated.)

7. In your own words, what was the point Paul wanted to make (vss. 15, 16, 21)?

8. If Paul and Peter both had the Holy Spirit living in them, how could they disagree? (They were influenced by their backgrounds, their friends, their personalities, their fears, etc.) **What are some disagreements among Christians today that might be explained in the same way?**

9. Do you know anyone who figures that, since faith and not following the law is what justifies us, sin is OK with Christ (vs. 17)? How would you respond to someone like that?

10. If Christ truly lives in us (vss. 18-20), how likely are we to abuse our Christian freedom? If every fifteen minutes you reminded yourself of Christ living in you, how do you think it would affect your relationships with friends? Family members? Teachers?

It can be hard to stand up for what's important while "turning the other cheek." Use the case studies on the reproducible sheet, "Let 'Em Have It?" to help kids think through which fights are worth fighting. Invite them to share similar situations they are struggling with. As you discuss their responses, remind them of these guidelines:

• Paul didn't let a problem slide if he saw that it might misrepresent the Gospel. (But sometimes making a scene *hurts* the credibility of your faith.)

• He didn't turn somebody *else's* cheek; he stood up for others when they were being mistreated.

LET 'EM HAVE IT ?

The Case of the Rude Wrestler

Yesterday in the school lunchroom one of the guys from the wrestling team grabbed your tray for himself, saying, "Hey, you're a Christian. You should be happy to let me have it." You were tempted to *really* "let him have it," especially when he added, "Besides, you're too much of a wimp to stop me." But it was only the Thursday Spam Surprise, and he *is* on the wrestling team. So, hey, maybe he needed it more than you did. But today he's eyeing your Hostess Twinkie and getting ready for an encore. What do you do?

The Case of the Cursing Chemist

The guy at the next bench in chemistry lab isn't having much success with his experiments—and even less success keeping his language clean. For weeks now you've been treated to a steady stream of swearing every time his beaker boils over. If it weren't for the fume hoods, you're sure the air would be blue. You don't feel right hearing the name of your Savior abused like that, but you don't want to give the impression that Christians are "holier than thou," either. What do you do?

The Case of the Cursing *Christian* Chemist

Same scenario as above, except: The cursing chemist claims to be a Christian. Now what do you do?

The Case of the Unfair Educator

Your biology teacher regularly puts down Christians for believing that God created the world. She's a lot better at expressing herself than you are, and you suspect she might make mincemeat out of any objections you could raise. Plus she's been known to put down more than just belief in Creation: rumor has it she also puts down—way down—the grades of those who disagree with her. What do you do?

GALATIANS 3

First Things First

The purpose of the Law was to point people to Jesus, not to serve as a means of attaining righteousness. But sometimes we get things backward by being justified first, and then trying to add new requirements for salvation.

Distribute copies of the reproducible sheet, "What's Going on Here?" and let kids find the errors. (The overall theme is that things are being done in the wrong order.) Explain that this chapter addresses what happens when you do two important things, but do them in the wrong order.

DATE I USED THIS SESSION _____ GROUP I USED IT WITH _____

NOTES FOR NEXT TIME _____

_____

_____

1. What's the most "foolish" thing you could do in a school classroom? On the football field? In the principal's office?

2. If you were a Galatian Christian reading verse 1, how would you feel? What would you want to tell Paul in return?

3. The Galatian Christians knew about Jesus' crucifixion and had believed in Him. But then they drifted back to their old way of worship—trying to be righteous based on keeping the Law rather than on trusting in Christ alone (vss. 1-5). **Why might that appeal to them?** (It was familiar; maybe salvation through faith alone seemed "too easy"; it's easier to control others with a set of rules than with a relationship, etc.)

4. Do you know people who seem more interested in rules, regulations, and outer appearances than in trusting Christ and being led by His Spirit? What are the biggest problems they face under such a system?

5. A lot of Jewish people pointed to Abraham as an example of building a relationship with God by what he did (especially circumcision). **Would you say that Abraham was justified (made right with God) because of what he did?** (Paul's response is in verses 6-9. God made the first move to build a relationship with Abraham, and all of Abraham's obedience was a response of gratitude and faith.)

6. The Old Testament Law was good in that it showed us what God expected. But no one could live up to it, so people were "cursed" (Deuteronomy 27:26). **How do we get out of that situation** (vss. 10-14)? (Jesus took our curse upon Himself and redeemed us. We can now live by faith and receive guidance from the Holy Spirit.)

7. If the Law were the only door to a good relationship with God, explains Paul, God wouldn't have waited 430 years (the time between Abraham and Moses) to provide it (vss. 15-20). **So is trying to do everything God says a waste of time** (vss. 21-25)? (Not at all! Obedience to God's commands is always desirable. Yet we place too much emphasis on the Law if we believe that's how we become righteous in God's eyes.)

8. The Law also divided people—it separated the "good" Jews from the "unholy" Gentiles. But faith in Jesus is open to anyone (vss. 26-29), so it brings people together. What are some things that tend to keep people apart today, even in some churches? (Age; skin color; financial status; knowledge of the Bible, etc.)

9. If we are "all one in Christ Jesus" (vs. 28), which of the following Christians do you need to get to know better: (a) those of a different race; (b) those who speak a different language; (c) those who worship differently; (d) those who are older or younger than you are (e) those who are richer or poorer than you are? How could you get to know these people better?

Tailor your discussion of this chapter to the needs of your group members. If they tend to be legalistic and think that they can—or have to—*earn* their way to heaven, help them see the futility of such an attempt by asking questions like: **Which of God's laws can you truly say you have never broken? Which have you broken?** Reread verse 10 and discuss the implications. Be sure group members know the true way to salvation. If, on the other hand, your group is a little too quick to toss aside God's commands, help them to see obedience as a response of gratitude and a mark (not the cause) of a right relationship with God.

WHAT'S GOING ON HERE?

GALATIANS 4

Come into the Family Room

Just as parents sometimes plan to provide certain things for their children, yet wait until the kids are old enough to handle the responsibility, so were God's people kept under the Law until Jesus came to give them freedom.

(Needed: Assortment of kids' favorite foods)

Before the meeting, prepare a spread of many of your group members' favorite foods. As the first kids arrive, explain that it's for them—but that they can't eat yet. When everyone gets there, assemble around the food and begin a general discussion (still not allowing anyone to nibble): **Is anyone hungry? Doesn't this stuff look good? What would you think of a starving person who came in and was offered this food, but didn't take it?** As you talk, periodically mention that it's not yet the right time to eat. After you've stalled for as long as you can, let kids chow down. Later, compare this experience with the "waiting period" under the Law that was ended with the coming of Jesus.

DATE I USED THIS SESSION _____ GROUP I USED IT WITH _____

NOTES FOR NEXT TIME _____

_____

_____

1. When did you first want your parents to stop thinking of you as a child? Do you think they have yet? Why or why not?

2. How do you think your relationship with your parents will change during the next five to ten years? (Let kids respond.) **Do you think the level of love your parents feel for you will change as you become more independent, move away, and maybe get married? Why?**

3. God's relationship with His people throughout history has been like a parent watching a child grow up (vss. 1-5). **What are some of the benefits of being God's children** (vss. 6, 7)**?** (We have His Spirit; we're no longer slaves to the Law; we become heirs as well.)

4. Suppose you have a teacher who's a nightmare for you. Your homework is triple that of other classes. He doesn't give *A's*. He lectures all the time. And your personality is exactly the opposite of his. You finally finish the course with a *D,* and you can't remember anything you were supposed to have learned. Next year you and your classmates must choose between this guy again or the Teacher of the Year. What would you think of anyone who chooses the terrible teacher? How is this like the situation of the Christians at Galatia (vss. 8-11)? **Explain.** (The Galatians were making an equally senseless decision to give up Christian freedom and go back to the "enslavement" of the Law.)

5. By deciding to return to the legalistic ways of the past, the Galatians were giving up the full joy that only Jesus can provide, but they were giving it up (vss. 12-16). **Why would they want to do that** (vss. 17-20)**?** (Probably out of fear. "Those people"—the Judaizers in Galatia—were misleading Christians. The false teaching may have included warnings of terrible eternal consequences for the Galatians if they didn't switch from grace to Law.)

6. As he had done in the last chapter, Paul again uses Abraham as an example (vss. 21-31). **On a scale where 12 years old is still a "slave," 18 is the initial stirrings of**

being free and independent, and 50 is maximum freedom, how "old" are you?

7. Which of the following is most like your reaction to all this talk about freedom in Christ—and why?

• The Christianity I know is about rules, not freedom.

• I wish somebody like Paul would tell my church or my parents that I need to be free to follow Jesus in my own way.

• I don't understand the whole subject.

• People today need more rules, not more freedom.

• Other (explain)

8. How could this group help you become more "free" in your relationship with God?

The reproducible sheet, "Slave Quarters or Family Room," will have kids consider some specific areas of Christian freedom and determine how "free" they feel in each area. After discussing their answers, make sure kids don't misunderstand the concept of freedom. It's easy to interpret "independence from the law" as "no need to obey rules." The next chapter of Galatians focuses on the need to "keep in step with the Spirit" to avoid this problem.

SLAVE QUARTERS or *FAMILY ROOM*

It's not always easy to feel comfortable around God. We're told to respect Him—to fear Him, even. When we think about the huge gap between our sinfulness and His perfection, we realize there's no way we can make up the difference.

But *He* can. Thanks to Jesus, those of us who put our faith in Him are entitled to all the rights and privileges God offers—to live in His "family room," so to speak. Yet many of us still feel stuck in the "slave quarters."

What "room" are you in when it comes to each of the following actions? Mark an X somewhere between "Slave Quarters" and "Family Room" to show how free you feel.

BEING HONEST WITH GOD ABOUT YOUR DOUBTS

Slave Quarters.........................Family Room

CALLING GOD "DADDY" (ABBA)

Slave Quarters.........................Family Room

BEING HONEST WITH GOD WHEN YOU'RE ANGRY

Slave Quarters.........................Family Room

INHERITING ALL THE BLESSINGS GOD HAS FOR YOU

Slave Quarters.........................Family Room

HAVING A SENSE OF HUMOR IN GOD'S PRESENCE

Slave Quarters.........................Family Room

ASKING GOD FOR ANYTHING

Slave Quarters.........................Family Room

PRAYING IN YOUR OWN WORDS

Slave Quarters.........................Family Room

EXPRESSING JOY ABOUT BELONGING TO GOD

Slave Quarters.........................Family Room

Are you trapped in the slave quarters when you could be in the family room? Remember, the freedom is yours, whether you feel that way or not. How can our group help you feel more at home in the family room?

Synchronized Stepping

We must never use our freedom in Christ as an excuse to indulge in sin; rather, we should "keep in step with the Spirit" and bear the Spirit's fruit.

(Needed: Seeds from various fruits; index cards; prize)

Give the group a "Fruit I.D. Test." Bring seeds you've taken from a variety of fruits—orange, apple, lemon, kiwi, strawberry, watermelon, etc. Display the seeds on index cards which you've placed on a table. Write a number on each card (from 1 to 10 if you have 10 kinds of seeds). Give each person paper and pencil and have each write down what kind of fruits the seeds are from. Whoever correctly identifies the most fruits wins a prize (perhaps some fruit-flavored bubble gum). Point out that you'll be talking about a very different kind of fruit in this session.

DATE I USED THIS SESSION _____ GROUP I USED IT WITH _____

NOTES FOR NEXT TIME_____

_____

_____

1. **When was the last time you felt really free?** (Examples: After completing a major assignment or a school year; when driving a car down the open highway, etc.)

2. **Can you have too much freedom?** (Too much free time with no plans or direction can lead to boredom. At first, summer vacation is sheer joy. But some students are ready to go back to school after a period of "doing nothing.")

3. **When you read the phrase, "Christ has set us free," what do you think of? Is this just a nice-sounding cliché, or has being a Christian really made you free in some way? Explain.**

4. **Why would anyone trade the freedom Christ gives for the chains of rules and regulations** (vs. 1)? (Maybe some don't "stand firm" against those who want everyone to fit into a system of rules. Or maybe they don't move forward in their spiritual development, and with "nothing to do," decide to go back to the only thing they know.)

5. **If your parent(s) offered you a brand new Porsche with no strings attached, how do you think they would feel if you kept riding your rusty old bike and working at your minimum wage job until you could buy a Porsche for yourself?** (They probably would be disappointed, hurt, and amazed at such a lack of sense.) **How do you think God feels when we reject His grace and keep trying to "earn" our right to be one of His** (vss. 2-5)?

6. **What's more important to God than your work, sweat, and sacrifice** (vs. 6)? (Faith and love.) **Which is easier to offer to God?** (Some people prefer to "put in hours" for God rather than let His love show through them to others every day.)

7. **The Galatians were being intentionally misled by a group of people (the Judaizers) who insisted on circumcision as a requirement for salvation, and the church had lost its joy. What would you do with people who mislead others in the name of religion?** (Let kids respond.) **What is the future of such people** (vss. 7-12)? (God will see that they will "pay the penalty." [Note in verse 12 what would be their "penalty" if Paul had his way.])

8. If you knew for certain that God would not punish you, which of the Ten Commandments might you break first? Or would you still try to obey every command in the Bible? What is your motivation for trying to obey God now?

9. If Christ has set you free, why not do as you please (vss. 13-21)? (Christ has set us free from slavery to sin—and free to serve Him out of love. We still struggle with our sinful natures, but as we learn to live by the Spirit, we feel less and less the desire to get involved with our old behaviors.)

10. If we consistently display the "fruit" of the Spirit (vss. 22, 23), do we even need the Law? Explain. (People who *always* display love, peace, self-control, etc., hardly need to be reminded, "Don't kill; don't steal; don't commit adultery.")

11. When people are marching and someone gets out of step, it's obvious. This is also true if we don't "keep in step with the Spirit" (vss. 24-26). What are some ways you would suggest for keeping in step? (Staying in step involves going in the same direction, not getting too far ahead or behind, not taking unnecessary stops or side trips, etc. In other words, it's always important to know what God expects of us and to stay faithful.)

The reproducible sheet, "In Step?" explores the specific "fruit of the Spirit." When group members finish, put them in three groups: School, Home, and Work. Go through the list and have groups provide an example of each quality "in action" at that location. If time permits, do the same thing with some of the specific "acts of the sinful nature" listed in verses 19-21 to use as a contrast.

▶ ▶ ▶ ▶ iN STEP ?

Some people don't care what God wants of them. Others become Christians, but start trying to "deserve" everything God gives them. Neither of these is a good way to relate to God.

It's far better to "keep in step with the Spirit" (Galatians 5:25). To see how well you're doing at this, fill in the footprints a little way, halfway, or all the way across to show how far you usually go in showing each quality. For example, if you think you model God's love at every opportunity God provides you, then color in the footprints all the way across the page.

▶ **LOVE – even to those you don't like**

▶ **JOY – even on a "bad hair" day**

▶ **PEACE – even during a surprise quiz**

▶ **PATIENCE – even with kids three grades below you**

▶ **KINDNESS – even to the "geek" most kids try not to be seen with**

▶ **GOODNESS – even when your parents aren't checking up on you**

▶ **FAITHFULNESS – in homework, chores, devotions**

▶ **GENTLENESS – especially to people weaker (or slower) than you are**

▶ **SELF-CONTROL – even when you have every reason to blow up or give in**

Sow So

Being a responsible Christian involves both "carrying one's own load" and helping to "carry each other's burdens." When we please God with our actions, we can look forward to a reward. But people who choose to please themselves instead of God can expect to "reap" destruction.

Have two volunteers act out the skit on the reproducible sheet, "Weed 'Em and Reap." Then discuss: **Have you heard the saying, "You'll reap what you sow"? What does it mean?** Observe that you'll be talking about that in this session.

DATE I USED THIS SESSION _____ GROUP I USED IT WITH _____

NOTES FOR NEXT TIME _____

_____

_____

1. You have a Christian best friend who suddenly dumps you and starts hanging around with a group that drinks all the time. You see him (or her) changing (for the worse) almost before your eyes. What do you do: (a) Forget about the person and find a new best friend; (b) go bawl the person out; (c) offer to go have a drink with the person and talk; or (d) something else? (Have kids explain their answers.)

2. Have you ever been "caught in a sin" (vs. 1) and had someone come "talk some sense into you"? If so, how did you feel about that person?

3. Do you think it's always possible to "restore the person gently"? Explain. If you try this and it doesn't work, what would you do next?

4. How might you "be tempted" (vs. 1) as you try to help someone? (You might get pulled into the same sin, especially if it's one you already have trouble resisting. That's why it's important to "watch yourself" and make sure you're really able to help.)

5. How do you "carry [someone's] burdens" (vs. 2)?

6. Do verses 2 and 5 disagree with each other? If each person is supposed to carry his or her own load, how can we also carry each other's burdens? (In the original language, the word used in verse 2 refers to a heavy load, and is in the context of spiritual temptation. In contrast, the word in verse 5 refers to a soldier's backpack. We should carry out our own responsibilities so that we can help those who are temporarily overburdened.)

7. When you think about how you're doing as a Christian, are you more likely to compare yourself to other people (vs. 4), or to something that the Bible says? Explain.

8. How do a lot of kids "sow to please [their] sinful nature" (vss. 7, 8)? What can they expect from their actions?

9. How do people sow "to please the Spirit"?

10. Do you know of Christians who have "become weary in doing good" (vss. 9, 10)? What has happened to such people? What do you think causes this? (Sometimes people don't pace themselves. Christianity is a lifelong marathon, not a sprint. If we try to do too much too quickly, we may discover that we're not rooted deeply enough in Scripture and in our relationship with God.)

11. Some people like to brag about themselves. Others boast of the people they've "brought to the Lord." Why did Paul "never boast except in the cross of our Lord Jesus Christ" (vss. 11-18)? (The cross was the most hated means of death known at the time. For Paul to "boast" in it was a reminder to follow Jesus' example of sacrificing for the sake of other people. We should all be so "boastful.")

Form small groups. Say: **How does your garden grow? We all "plant" something with our actions. Some of us plant selfish "seeds" (through drinking, drugs, sex, rebellion, etc). Others "sow to please the Spirit," and grow love, joy, peace, self-control, and other good fruit. Look again at the list of fruit in Galatians 5:22, 23. Then look at the "weed" list in Galatians 5:19-21. Tell the others in your small group two kinds of fruit that you need to plant or cultivate—and two kinds of weeds that you need to pull out right away.**

WEED 'EM AND REAP

Characters:
Salesperson, customer
Place: A garden supply store

SALESPERSON *(standing behind counter):* Good afternoon. Welcome to the Weed 'Em and Reap Garden Center. How may I—

CUSTOMER *(angrily):* Don't change the subject. I'm mad, and it's all your fault!

SALESPERSON: What seems to be the problem?

CUSTOMER: It's these cucumber seeds. I planted them, and cucumbers came up!

SALESPERSON: Uh. . . So what's the problem?

CUSTOMER: I hate cucumbers! They make me burp! I play the tuba in the school band, and if I start burping during a concert, it spoils everything!

SALESPERSON: But if you didn't want cucumbers, why did you plant cucumber seeds?

CUSTOMER: Because they're so easy to plant. They're not big and ugly like pumpkin seeds. Or tiny and hard to hold like carrot seeds. They're just right.

SALESPERSON: But if you plant cucumber seeds, you get cucumber. If you plant radish seeds, you get radish. If you plant beet seeds, you get beet.

CUSTOMER: Beat, eh? Don't threaten me! I want my money back!

SALESPERSON *(sighing):* Here's what I'll do. You tell me what you wanted to grow, and I'll give you the seeds to grow it.

CUSTOMER: Spaghetti.

SALESPERSON: Pardon me?

CUSTOMER: Spaghetti. I wanted to grow spaghetti.

SALESPERSON: But spaghetti doesn't grow from seeds.

CUSTOMER: Don't try to tell *me* about gardening. I play the tuba!

SALESPERSON *(wearily):* Right. OK. Here are some spaghetti seeds. It says "Onions" on the package, but it's really spaghetti.

CUSTOMER: It's about time! I can't afford to waste another dollar on seeds. They're too expensive. *(Exiting)* Money doesn't grow on trees, you know!

SALESPERSON *(thinking):* It doesn't?

EPHESIANS 1

Making the Blest of It

We have a lot of things to praise God for. Foremost among them is His Son, Jesus Christ, who provides everything we need to live in unity as Christians. Jesus has been placed at the right hand of God above all other things, and is the head of His body, the church.

Explain to kids that you're going to call out a number (five, for instance). They're to get in groups of that number (five kids per group, for instance). Each group must sit back-to-back on the floor, link arms, and stand up. Each member of the first group that stands wins a point for that round. Anyone who doesn't get in a group loses a point for that round. Conclude the game by getting everyone linked together and trying to stand up. (If your group is too small for this game, have pairs compete to see which can first form the *shape* [by lying down and positioning arms, etc.] of a number you call out.) Then explain that this chapter describes God's purpose as linking all things together under Christ (vs. 10).

DATE I USED THIS SESSION _____ GROUP I USED IT WITH _____

NOTES FOR NEXT TIME _____

_____

_____

1. If someone offered you a new mansion in the design of your choice, any car you want, and a million dollars, would there be any reason you would turn down the offer? Explain. (Possibilities: Wondering what the "catch" was; not wanting to change lifestyles, etc.)

2. What are some things that you think are more important than cars, homes, and money? (Let kids respond.) When you read that God provides "every spiritual blessing" (vss. 1-3), what things come to your mind?

3. When was the last time someone made you feel important? Describe the situation. (Compare responses to being chosen by God to be His people [vss. 4-6].)

4. True or false: Since faith is necessary for being a Christian, we don't need to understand what God is doing in our lives. Explain. (See verses 7-10. While there are many things we may need to accept on faith, God still makes available wisdom, understanding, and knowledge of the mystery of His will. Blind faith might be "the easy way around" study and knowledge of things we *can* know.)

5. Do you have a philosophy of life, or some kind of master plan for what you want to accomplish? If so, what is it? How do your goals compare with God's master plan "to bring all things in heaven and on earth together under one head, even Christ" (vs. 10)?

6. How should God's "master plan" affect your plans in the following areas: (a) the way you treat enemies; (b) the way you relate to non-Christian friends; (c) the kind of job you try to get? (Answers will vary, but in general we should find our place "under" Christ and live for Him in a way that attracts as many to Him as possible. And since God is trying to bring all things together, we should also be more accepting of others.)

7. How can you be sure that you'll get all the things God has promised (vss. 11-14)? (Just as someone might convince a landlord that he or she will pay the rent by providing two months' worth in advance, God gives His people the Holy Spirit as a deposit to guarantee our inheritance.)

8. What parts of Paul's prayer for his fellow Christians (vss. 15-19) **do you regularly include in your prayers? What elements would you like to start including?**

9. **Think for a moment about Jesus as He's usually described in the Gospels—a submissive servant. Then read the description of Him in verses 19-23. Why do you think there is such a difference?** (Jesus had a specific job to do while He was on earth, which He carried out. But after completing His work, He was reunited with the Father and rewarded.)

10. **How does Christ's power benefit you right now? What will it do for you in the future?**

(Needed: Thumbtack or brass fastener)

Before the session, cut the wheel and spinner from a copy of the reproducible sheet, "Wheel of Blessings." (If you can copy the sheet onto heavy paper, or glue the wheel and spinner to light cardboard, the spinner will work more smoothly.) Attach the spinner to the wheel with a thumbtack or brass fastener. Begin the activity be asking kids to share areas in their lives where they need God's help—peace at home, more self-confidence, healing in a relationship, etc. (If your kids are uncomfortable with this level of openness, invite them to list areas in which they think many people their age would like help.) As each challenge is mentioned, have the person who mentioned it spin the spinner. Point out that the "Wheel of Blessings" is random, but God's help isn't; He provides us with what we need. When the spinner points to a blessing, discuss how people could claim and apply that blessing to the particular problem. After several problems have been discussed, spend some time in prayer—first focusing on who Jesus is and what He has done for us, and then asking Him to provide everything needed for group members to make a difference in the world around them.

WHEEL OF BLESSINGS

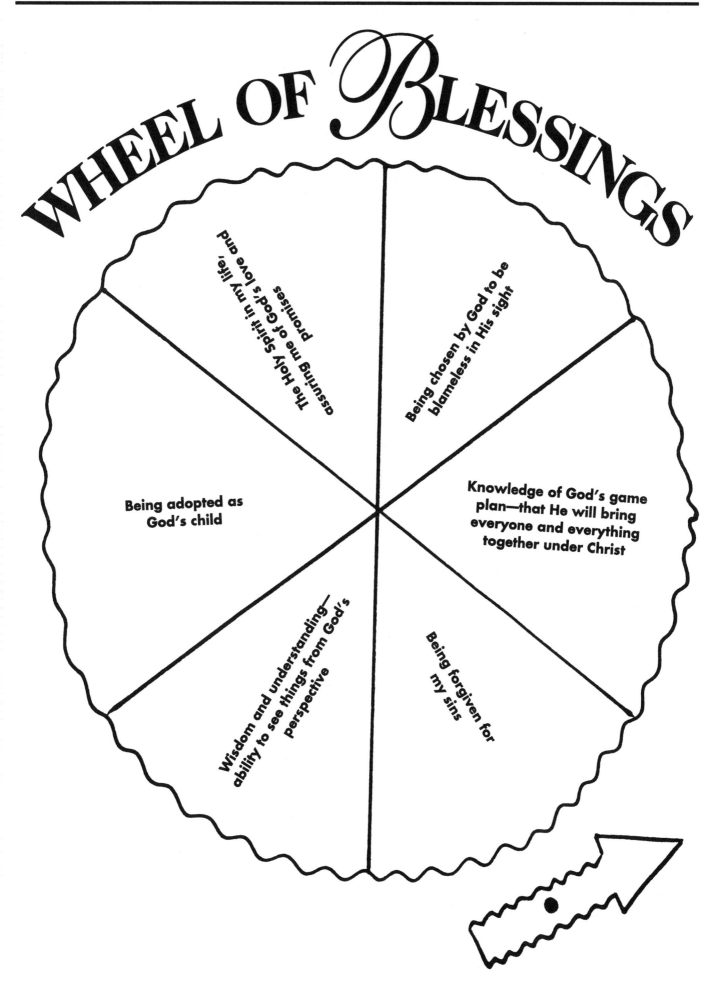

Being chosen by God to be blameless in His sight

The Holy Spirit in my life, assuring me of God's love and promises

Being adopted as God's child

Knowledge of God's game plan—that He will bring everyone and everything together under Christ

Wisdom and understanding— ability to see things from God's perspective

Being forgiven for my sins

Works Don't Work

We can't work our way into God's kingdom; we can only receive His free gift through our faith. Jews, Gentiles—all who believe in Jesus qualify as "fellow citizens" and "members of God's household."

Play the game "Red Rover." Two equal teams stand facing each other, holding hands. Team one calls to team two, "Red Rover, Red Rover, let so-and-so come over." The person called must try to break through the opposing team's line. If the person succeeds, he or she may bring someone back to his or her team. If the person fails, he or she joins the team that called him or her. The team with the most members after a set amount of time wins. Explain that this chapter tells how Christ broke down the barrier between formerly opposing sides.

DATE I USED THIS SESSION _____ GROUP I USED IT WITH _____

NOTES FOR NEXT TIME _____

_____

_____

1. Have you ever had a bad habit that you tried to stop "cold turkey"? Has anyone you know done this? What motivated this change of behavior? (A "close call"; seeing a friend or family member suffer from the same habit; an intellectual decision to make a change, etc.) **What's the hardest thing about stopping something "cold turkey"?** (Being addicted [physically or psychologically] to the habit; going through "withdrawal," etc.)

2. Why can't all the people in the world just "stop sinning—cold turkey" (vss. 1-3)? (We are born into sin, we are led into sin by Satan, and we have sinful cravings. We are, in fact, "dead" in our sins, and death is something we don't decide to undo with a "cold turkey" decision. Christ is the only One who can bring us to life and help us throw off the chains of sin.)

3. What are some things you received—maybe from your parents or friends—without earning them at all? How did you respond? We receive salvation by God's grace, or undeserved favor (vss. 4-9). How do you respond to God for that gift?

4. How important are the "works" that we perform (vs. 10)? (As a substitute for God's grace, a way of "earning" salvation, they're worthless. Yet in response to God's grace and our salvation, our whole purpose in life should be to work for God.)

5. Has anyone ever tried to keep you out of a clique or other group? How did you feel? (Let kids respond.) How do you think Jewish and Gentile people felt about each other during the time described in verses 11 and 12? (The Jews had been God's chosen people, and the Gentiles [non-Jewish people] were outsiders. But when Jesus died, He made salvation possible for everyone. [See verse 13.])

6. Since Jesus "destroyed the barrier" (vss. 14-18) between the Jews and Gentiles—people who were violently opposed to each other—what should be your attitude toward Jewish people today? (There's no place for anti-Semitism—or any other form of discrimination based on selfish pride or hate—in Christianity.)

7. What was the cost to Jesus of breaking down this barrier? (He gave His life.) How far are you willing to go to break down barriers between opposing groups in your school?

8. Together, Christians compose a "building"—a holy temple for God (vss. 19-22). Jesus is the cornerstone. What part of the building do you think you are? Explain. (Examples: "Floor boards" could provide support for others; "beams" could handle large amounts of stress; "windows" could help others see clearly; etc.)

9. Since Jesus made you alive, what are some of the "cravings of [the] sinful nature" (vs. 3) that you're trying to leave behind you in the "cemetery"?

The reproducible sheet, "One Way or Two?" helps kids visualize the "faith" and "works" approaches to salvation. Let volunteers show and explain their drawings. Follow with a short review of how to receive Christ as Savior, and give kids an opportunity to put their faith in Him. Then brainstorm some "good works" kids can do as a group—not to earn God's favor, but to show others that God's "workmanship" (vs. 10) has not been wasted.

ONE WAY
OR TWO?

"For it is by grace you have been saved, through faith—and this not from yourselves, it is the gift of God—not by works, so that no one can boast" (Ephesians 2:8, 9).

For a few minutes, think of good actions—loving others, giving to those in need, etc.—as cars on the road of life. Cars are important—but not as important as the road you're on.

Label the cars on the dead-end road with actions people might take to try to earn their way to heaven—perfectly good things like going to church, or helping the homeless.

On the one-way street, draw your own picture of how we receive salvation. (You might want to involve a cross, or even show Jesus tearing up the "tickets" you should have gotten.) Then label the cars on this road with actions you can take to show that you are God's workmanship.

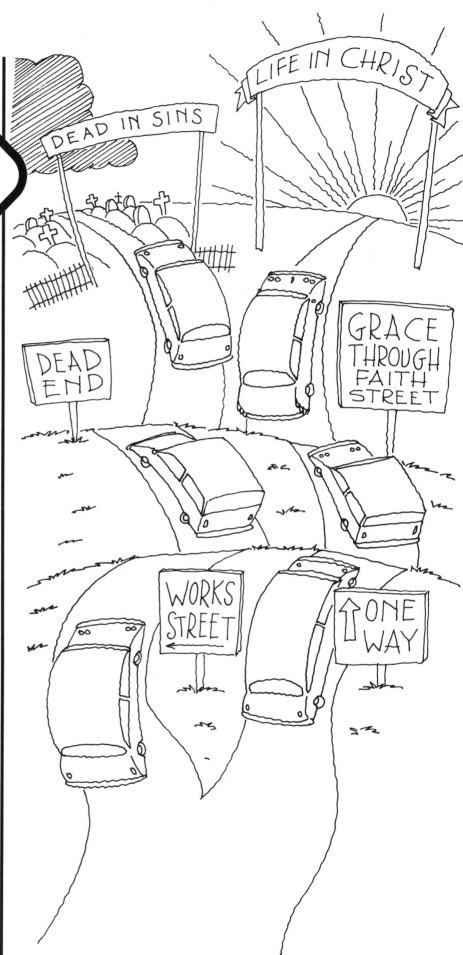

EPHESIANS 3

Fill 'Er Up

God's tremendous grace is reflected in His acceptance of the Gentiles into His kingdom. Paul prays that all believers would be filled with the love and power of God, who is able to do even more than we ask for or imagine.

(Needed: Prize)

Distribute copies of the reproducible sheet, "Only You," and read through the directions. After kids have completed the sheets, find out who gave the greatest number of unique answers. Give that person a prize for being "most like nobody else." Then explain that Paul's long-term mission was like nobody else's: to take the Gospel to the Gentiles.

DATE I USED THIS SESSION _____ GROUP I USED IT WITH _____

NOTES FOR NEXT TIME _____

_____

_____

1. What motivates you to keep going when you face a tough challenge in school? In sports? In a relationship? (Drive to succeed; focusing on the desired result, etc.)

2. What parts of Paul's lifestyle, with all the rejection and suffering as well as joy, would you choose for yourself? Which parts wouldn't you want? What if you had to take "all or nothing"? (Some kids might want Paul's closeness to God. They aren't likely to volunteer to go through all he did, though.) **What do you think motivated Paul to keep going in spite of the obstacles he faced (vs. 1)?** (He'd come to think of himself as a "prisoner" of Jesus. Paul's own selfish wants were insignificant.)

3. It's often hard for us to understand what God is doing—especially when we're going through a tough time. Looking back, can you think of a time when God used a negative experience to bring about something better? How does that compare to verses 1-6? (Paul reminds us that the Gentiles had always been outsiders when it came to religious things [vss. 1-6]. But at last Jesus opened the way for everyone—Jews and Gentiles alike—to be reconciled with God. God's "mystery" then became clear.)

4. When the time is right, we need to make the most of our opportunities. When have you gotten something good by being "in the right place at the right time"? (Examples: Winning a contest; finding a rare rock or arrowhead on the ground; running into a friend you hadn't seen in a long time, etc.) **How would Paul have answered this question (vss. 7-13)?** (Though he considered himself "less than the least of all God's people," Paul was used by God to carry the Gospel to the Gentiles—because the time was right.)

5. Who are some people you know who might respond to the love and forgiveness of God—yet as far as you know, no one has talked to them about Christ? Is there some way you could bring up the subject with them?

6. Because of Jesus, "we may approach God with freedom and confidence" (vs. 12). On a scale of 1 (least) to 10 (most), how confident do you feel to talk to God about absolutely anything?

7. If you know a lot about Jesus, are you all set to go to work for Him (vss. 14-19)? Explain. (Not necessarily. First we need His power and to know, to some degree, how much He loves us. His love surpasses knowledge. Lots of people know *about* Jesus, but don't actually know *Him.)*

8. Would you say that you've experienced the "depth" of Jesus' love? Or would it be more truthful to say only that you know He's a loving God? Explain.

9. How wide, long, high, and deep *is* the love of Christ? How would you explain this to a six-year-old child?

10. Do you think Jesus is ever annoyed by our requests? Why? (See verses 20 and 21. Sometimes our requests might be selfishly motivated, and would not be pleasing to God. Yet when we have heartfelt concerns and genuine spiritual needs, God is ready and able to provide more than we ask for—even more than we can imagine.)

11. What's the most amazing thing you can imagine God doing for you? Are you willing to ask Him to do that? Why or why not?

Say: **Let's say something happens to this group tonight. Each of us is filled with Christ's love and power in a way that we've never known before. We're no longer afraid of anything. What would be the first thing you would do? What would be different about our next meeting? What project could we take on that had seemed impossible before?** As kids respond, try to help them see how fear keeps us from being all God wants us to be. As they come up with "impossible" projects, remind them that God is able to do even more. Spend time praying together about knowing more of Christ's power and love, and asking God to help kids overcome specific fears they have.

 ONLY YOU

Directions: For each of these categories, list something you think nobody else in this group will have in common with you. (For example, if your parents are immigrants from another country, you could list that for the first category.) You'll get one point for each entry that nobody else matches.

1

Something unique about your family

. . . .
. . . .

2

Place you've gone on vacation that nobody else has gone

. . . .
. . . .

3

Hobby that nobody else has

. . . .
. . . .

4

Sport you've tried that nobody else has tried

. . . .
. . . .

5

Food you've eaten that nobody else has eaten

. . . .
. . . .

6

Strange, unique habit someone in your family has

. . . .
. . . .

7

Something unique about your appearance

. . . .
. . . .

8

Something you're good at that no one else is good at

. . . .
. . . .

9

Book you've read that nobody else has read

. . . .
. . . .

10

Radio station you've listened to that nobody else has

. . . .
. . . .

EPHESIANS 4

Hanging Together

Because there is one Lord, we should be of one mind. This means we need to be patient and bear with each other, to use our gifts for the good and unity of the church, and to watch what we say and how we say it.

Have kids get in teams of equal number (preferably not their usual cliques). Tell them that you'll name a category; each team must come up with three things in that category on which all its members agree. Agreement must be unanimous within each team. The first team to do so wins the round. Sample categories might include: admired sports figures; favorite TV shows; detested foods; favorite candy bars, etc. In some cases teams might not be able to answer—if, for example, one team member never watches TV. In such cases, the team is unable to win. This activity can prepare kids for the subject of unity in the church.

DATE I USED THIS SESSION _____ GROUP I USED IT WITH _____

NOTES FOR NEXT TIME _____

_____

_____

1. If you got a phone call from the President of the United States, personally asking you to serve on his Committee to Improve Literacy among Young People, would you take him up on it? When you went to your first meeting, how would you dress? How would you feel deep down inside?

2. As a Christian, you have a "calling" from God (vss. 1, 2). How do you feel about it? Is being a Christian something you feel a need to be "worthy" of, or are you sometimes a little embarrassed to admit it to some people?

3. What are some things that Christians strongly debate (or perhaps even fight about)? God's goal for His people is unity (vss. 2-6). Does that mean when you disagree with another Christian you should give in? Explain. (It's clear that we're to remain humble, gentle, patient, and loving. We need to be willing to admit when we're wrong. At other times, when dealing with issues where no clear answer is evident, a *loving* expression of opinion is good.)

4. Let's say someone from a non-Christian religion quotes verse 6 to you and says, "See? God is everybody's Father. All faiths lead to the same God." What would you say? (The body and Spirit [vs. 4] are Christ's, so the "all" in verse 6 refers only to those who belong to Christ.])

5. One challenge to maintaining unity is realizing that other people have gifts we don't have, and vice versa (vss. 7-13). You may not know exactly what spiritual gift(s) you have. But you might have some idea. What do you think your gift(s) might be? Do you see certain spiritual strengths among other people in the group?

6. Which is harder for you: speaking the truth even when it makes you uncomfortable, or being loving when you say what you think (vs. 15)? Why?

7. Verse 16 says that each of us, in his or her own way, helps hold the whole body together. Do your friendships in this group tend to keep the group together? Or do they tend to separate you from the rest of the group? Explain.

8. If we don't choose to live as Christians, what choice is left to us (vss. 17-19)? (We harden ourselves to God's calling and must follow our own sensual desires, which are never satisfied.)

9. How does a relationship with Jesus keep us from falling into such a desperate way of life (vss. 20-24)? (He helps us to "put off" the old, sinful self and "put on" the new self so we can have a God-given desire for righteousness.)

10. What's the longest you've ever stayed mad at someone? How would things have been different if you'd followed the instruction in verses 26 and 27?

11. If you knew a guy who was just getting out of a "youth correctional center" after serving time for stealing cars, how could you help him obey verse 28?

Perhaps the most difficult command from this chapter for young people is the warning against unwholesome talk (vs. 29). The reproducible sheet, "Gross or Glowing?," gives you a way to get into that subject. Cut a copy of the sheet into the four speakers' parts. Have each part read aloud by a volunteer as if it were made up of perfectly normal sentences. After each reading, ask how group members feel. Chances are that the positive words in readings 1 and 3 will leave them feeling better than readings 2 and 4. Read verses 29-32 and ask: **How do your words usually leave others feeling? How do you think they leave God feeling? Are your words more like verse 31 or verse 32 at home? At school? In this group?** As a group, design a system that will help kids monitor "unwholesome talk" in the group. (For example, for every insult recorded by someone, three compliments will cancel it out. Or perhaps a nickel "fine" for every offense could be collected, with the proceeds going for group parties.) Given the opportunity, most kids will come up with something creative—which can keep them thinking about this issue for weeks to come.

SPEAKER 1

Shining happy good? Sure, plenty great wonderful success. Amazing constructive praising, brand new nice-smelling healthy. Improved number one blue ribbon, beautiful grand sincerely.

SPEAKER 2

Miserable sickly gross! Trash garbage rotten, smelly dead failure. Horrible dirty awful mistake, stupid illegal decaying. Scum slime angry criminal fighting? Hate.

SPEAKER 3

Fantastic buildup wow! Heavenly delicious, golden talented exciting. Glowing warm laughter? Always faithful love, gentle genuine 100 percent together, friendship reward. Colorful high-flying Bible treat, yes I promise.

SPEAKER 4

Idiot never has-been flop? Sinful wrong violent dummy, sleazy hassle bruise. Cancer moron poison broken, slavery dying rejection slap. Hurt harmful danger collapse, disease disaster moldy dope bacteria germs.

EPHESIANS 5

Light, Not Lite

Christians are "children of light." As such, we should make sure that our actions reflect the God we serve. Anything that even hints of sin needs to be wiped away as each of us becomes filled with the Holy Spirit. One of the main areas in which we should model God's love is in marriage relationships.

(Needed: A candle for each person; matches)

Form two teams. Give each person a candle, and find a large open area, approximately square (outside works well). One team should prepare to walk north to south, and the other east to west. The first team to get all its members to the other end of the room or yard will win—but no one can move unless his or her candle is burning. To begin, light the candle of one person on each team at the same time. That person then passes along the flame to fellow team members as quickly as possible. (Anyone with a lit candle can light someone else's.) Kids then try to cross the room or yard. If a candle goes out, that person must "freeze" until it is relit. Of course, as team members begin to crisscross, they can help "encourage" opposing team members' candles to go out. This activity leads into the idea that Jesus, "the light," makes us alive, as kids will see in this chapter.

DATE I USED THIS SESSION _____ GROUP I USED IT WITH _____

NOTES FOR NEXT TIME _____

_____

_____

1. Have you ever been fooled by an imitation that looked real? (Examples: Counterfeit money; a plastic egg, apple, or other food item; novelty items like fake blood; celebrity lookalikes, etc.)

2. Sometimes imitating is a great thing to do. What skills have you learned by imitating someone else?

3. As Christians, we're all supposed to "be imitators of God" (vss. 1, 2). How is it possible to imitate someone we've never seen? (We know many of God's qualities from the way He's described in the Bible. And we have a good record of Jesus, who said, "Anyone who has seen me has seen the Father" [John 14:9].)

4. What happens when Christians don't imitate God? (It sends mixed signals to those around them. To call yourself a "child of God" and then commit sin whenever you feel like it damages the image of all Christians—not to mention God's reputation.)

5. Look at some of the specific sins that are mentioned (vss. 3-7). Which of them do you think is easiest for people your age to fall into? Why?

6. Paul contrasts the "shady deals" of sin with the brightness of Christ's light (vss. 8-14). Christians, as "children of light," should be uncovering and removing sin, rather than hiding it. How should you "expose" the "deeds of darkness" in your school? In this group? (By living as children of light, thereby showing the contrast between good and evil. It's not a matter of rooting out other people's sins and shining a spotlight on them; it's a matter of showing sin for what it is by setting a good example [vss. 12, 13].)

7. Christians have their share of problems. But people who are slaves to sin have no real, lasting solutions to look forward to. One common "substitute solution" is to get drunk and forget problems for a while. What are some differences you would expect to see between someone who's under the influence of alcohol and someone who's under the influence of the Spirit (vss. 15-21)?

8. When you sing "psalms, hymns, and spiritual songs," do you really "speak to" those around you (vs. 19)? To God? Or do you tend to say the words without really communicating to anyone? How would you explain this to Paul?

9. Some people read the next passage in Ephesians (vss. 22-33) **and think that the idea of a wife submitting to her husband is unfair and sexist. Do you? Explain.** (Submission is voluntarily yielding your will to another person's out of respect. It doesn't mean that you let yourself be manipulated or abused. Submission to each other is to be standard practice among all Christians [vs. 21], and a wife's submission is only one example. Point out that if husbands "love [their] wives, just as Christ loved the church," submission shouldn't cause a problem. Jesus submitted Himself to the will of the Father, but He was not "inferior" to the Father.)

Read verse 18 again. Help kids see that being filled with the Holy Spirit really can meet the needs that many young people hope drinking will meet. Read the case studies on the reproducible sheet, "Under the Influence." As a group, think through why each person might be turning to alcohol. (Examples: Desire to fit in; need to handle stress, etc. Explore the issue rather than going for a single "right" answer.) Then discuss how the power of the Holy Spirit and a right relationship with God could better help meet those needs. (If you sense a group member has a problem with alcohol, follow up individually later.)

Under the Influence

Six-Pack

Thank goodness it's Friday! Brian has had a killer week: two tests and a major paper due, plus the big game coming up tomorrow. The coach has been on his case all week, as if it's totally up to Brian whether they win or lose. But finally school and practice are over, and he's got some time to hang out with his friends. Probably they'll get a couple of six-packs, drive somewhere, and just kick back.

Party Time

Heather checks her makeup in the rearview mirror one more time before getting out of the car. She's been seeing Andy for a few weeks now, but they've never really done anything with his friends before tonight. She hopes she's dressed right for this party—not too casual, but not exactly like she's going to hang out at the mall, either. As she and Andy go into the house, she looks around to see how many people she knows. Not too many; this really isn't her crowd. She thinks it'll be fun, though, as she takes the beer Andy hands her.

Home Alone

Paul cautiously turns down the volume on his CD player. It sounds like everything is quiet downstairs again. He looks out his bedroom window; sure enough, there goes Mom, squealing out of the driveway on her way to who-knows-where. Dad must have left already—probably back to the bar for the rest of the night. Oh, well, at least there won't be any more fighting tonight. With the house to himself for a while, Paul heads down to the kitchen, mixes himself a drink from the liquor cabinet, and settles in front of the TV to spend another night home alone.

Power Struggles

If we really learn to put God first in our lives, our other relationships take on new meaning. Obedience to parents and productivity at work are no longer burdens, but by-products of trying to serve God wholeheartedly. As we face more serious (spiritual) challenges, we should realize that God equips us with the "armor" needed to protect us.

(Needed: "Weapons" for a fun fight)

Indulge your kids in the kind of fun fight they like best. (If facilities allow, try squirt gun or water balloon fights. Other fun weapons are nylon stockings stuffed with clothing, or pillows.) Pit guys against girls or form any other teams that will get rivalry going. When you get everybody settled down again, explain that this chapter talks about fights with parents and other authorities—and about a fight we need powerful weapons for.

DATE I USED THIS SESSION _____ GROUP I USED IT WITH _____

NOTES FOR NEXT TIME _____

_____

_____

1. If and when you become a parent, what are you going to do differently from your folks?

2. What are some common ways that teenage girls don't honor or obey their parents (vss. 1-3)? How about teenage guys?

3. If a parent does something to "exasperate" you, which he or she is commanded not to do (vs. 4), do you think that cancels out the instruction for you to be obedient? Explain. (Both commands—for children to obey and for fathers to not exasperate—are independent of the other's response.)

4. Have you had a bad working situation that you can tell us about? How do you feel about Paul's commands in verses 5-9? Do you think you might be able to improve a bad situation if you followed this advice? What motivation would you have to be a good worker even if it didn't improve your situation? (God will eventually reward us, even if our boss doesn't.)

5. When and where do you feel strongest as a Christian (vs. 10)? When and where do you feel weakest?

6. Which of the following do you think is one of "the devil's schemes" (vs. 11)? Which would be most likely to lead you into sinning? Why?

• A teacher tells your class to read a book that contains a couple of sexual scenes.

• A coach tells your football team to "hit 'em where it hurts."

• A friend tells you that she knows how to get an advance copy of a big test.

7. How do we "struggle" against the devil (vs. 12)? Isn't is just a fact that all people sin, and when we do we turn to God for forgiveness? (Every sin is a "loss" in our spiritual struggle. We face frequent temptation, and we need to "fight" to keep from giving in. While God will forgive our wrongdo-

169

ing, it's much better to let Him act in our lives *before* we lose a battle.)

8. **What would you think of a football player who refused to wear his pads and helmet in a big game? Would that show how tough and independent he was? Explain.** (It would only show how foolish he was, and he would almost be asking to get hurt.) **Do you ever try to fight temptation unarmed? If so, why?**

9. **Which piece of "armor" with which God equips us for our spiritual battles** (vss. 13-18) **protects your back?** (No such protection is provided. We are equipped to stand and fight temptations that come our way. [Of course, when the choice is ours, we should "flee" from potentially harmful situations.])

The reproducible sheet, "The Best Offense," further examines the "armor of God." When group members finish, have volunteers show some of their armor. Ask: **Judging from the sizes of your pieces of armor, what do you most need to work on?** Then have each person think of a current "battle" he or she is fighting with a human, not with the devil. Explain that if such conflicts aren't quickly resolved, both parties are open to the temptation to hate, get revenge, become bitter, or hold a grudge. Challenge kids to wrap up those conflicts (wherever possible) and devote their energies to the real battle—the spiritual one.

They say the best offense is a good defense. God gives us all the equipment we need to take our stand against "the devil's schemes." The problem is, some of us aren't "suiting up" completely before we go into battle.

For instance, take the "sword of the Spirit, which is the word of God" (Ephesians 6:17). If you don't know much about the Bible, your "sword" may not be any bigger than a toothpick.

THE BEST OFFENSE

Let's say the person below is you. You'll also see the "armor" available to you, in the correct proportional size. To show how "equipped" you are for battle, "put on" the items by drawing them on the figure. But draw them in a size that shows how much you depend on them when you're tempted. (For example, if you're always truthful, but don't have a lot of faith, draw your belt very large and your shield very small.)

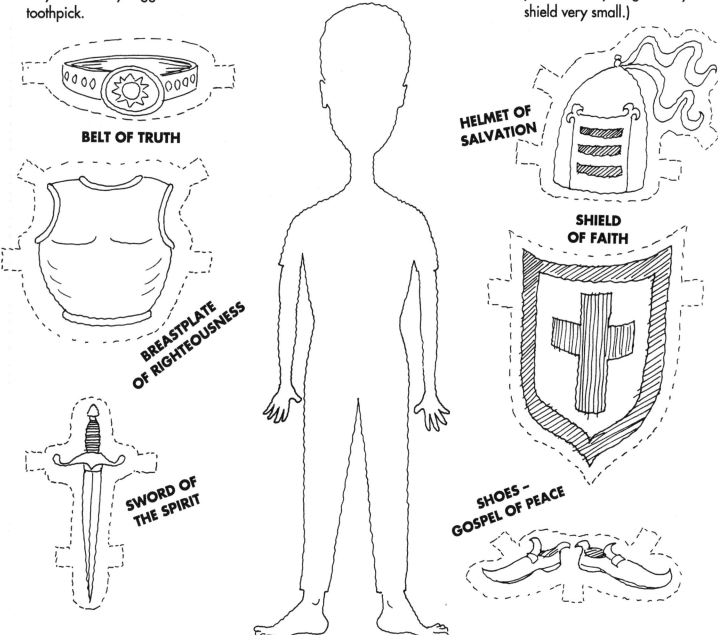

BELT OF TRUTH

BREASTPLATE OF RIGHTEOUSNESS

SWORD OF THE SPIRIT

HELMET OF SALVATION

SHIELD OF FAITH

SHOES – GOSPEL OF PEACE